Eve
from the
Autobiography
and
Other Poems

EVE

from the Autobiography
and Other Poems

Betsy Colquitt

Introduction by James Ward Lee

A Center for Texas Studies Book

Texas Christian University Press
Fort Worth

Library of Congress Cataloging-in-Publication Data

Colquitt, Betsy Feagan.
  Eve—from the autobiography, and other poems / Betsy
Colquitt.
      p. cm.
    ISBN 0-87565-174-7 (alk. paper)
    1. Eve (Biblical figure)—poetry. 2. Women—poetry.
I. Title.
PS3553.P4766E94 1997
811′.54-dc21
                                      97019118
                                          CIP

Design by Barbara Whitehead
Cover photo, "Santa Elena Canyon," from
Where Rainbows Wait for Rain: The Big Bend Country,
photographs by Richard Fenker Jr. and poems by Sandra Lynn.
Courtesy of the photographer.

For Landon Augustus Colquitt (1919-1991)

and our daughters,

Clare and Kate

Acknowledgments

This book owes its existence to James Ward Lee of the Center for Texas Studies at the University of North Texas, who envisioned the collection and guided me in its realization. I'm grateful to him, to the Center for Texas Studies, which joins Texas Christian University Press in publishing this volume, and to many others, among them Judy Alter, director, and Tracy Row, editor, of TCU Press for their care to editorial and publication details; Barbara Whitehead for designing this volume; Richard Fenker Jr. for allowing use of his *Santa Elena Canyon* photograph; Jerry Bradley, who in 1982 as editor of Saurian Press issued *Honor Card*, here reprinted with minor changes; and to editors of the journals and anthologies below in which many poems collected here and now revised first appeared:

Approach, The Builder and the Dream, Christian Century, Concho River Review, Crucible, English in Texas, Fiction and Poetry by Texas Women, Forum, The Goliards, Gulf Coast Collection of Stories & Poems, Ilzes Pasaule 1928-1981, Latitude 30° 18', New and Experimental Literature, New Laurel Review, New Mexico Humanities Review, New Texas 91, New Texas 95, The Pawn Review, Pilgrimage, Poet—An International Monthly, Quartet, riverSedge, Sam Houston Literary Review, Sands, Southwest: A Contemporary Anthology, The Texas Anthology, Texas in Poetry: A 150-Year Anthology, This Place of Memory: A Texas Perspective, Vanderbilt Review, Vision.

Though *Eve—from the Autobiography and Other Poems* draws on more sources than I can acknowledge, I am aware of my debt to many teachers—writers, artists, colleagues, students and friends. Predictably perhaps, my greatest debts are to my parents, Belton Dial Feagan and Eddie Young Feagan, and to my husband, daughters and grandsons.

Contents

HONOR CARD AND OTHER POEMS

Honor Card, Part Four

UNCOLLECTED AND NEW POEMS

Migrants

thinking of *the potato eaters*

The Terrible Peaceable Kingdom

no-fault divorce

Back

Introduction

By James Ward Lee

Good poetry makes the familiar seem new. True poetry must, as Pope says of true wit, tell us "what oft was thought but ne'er so well expressed." The poems in Betsy Colquitt's *Eve—from the Autobiography and Other Poems* do exactly that—and more. Not only are the "oft thought" things in Colquitt's poetry "well expressed," but the "Eve" poems even offer new thoughts. New in that the author turns the stories we learned from Genesis—and, in more cases than may be healthy, from Milton—upside down. Adam is no longer the first human on earth. Eve is. Eve names the plants and animals, invents the wheel, baskets, pottery. And then Eve finds Adam in the strange soil of Eden:

> suddenly this strange soil breeding
> scarabs quickens, gives
> as finger comes forth and i take it,
> hand, arm coming free of burying earth
> . . . .
> he is clay-coated and ugly,
> his strange umbilical linked still
> to his source. unwife
> i discover midwifery.

And then Eve "informs him our geography," "teaches him my language," and names him: "*ādām* i say, *man*,"

In the beginning, Eve awakens in the garden and begins making sense of the world in which she finds herself. By naming things around her and by naming herself, she helps to create herself. Naming things, discovering things, inventing things, awakening to the world, Eve seeing her image in a stream says, "*eve,* i say, *hawwa, the living one,* and i am" ("am-ing"). And from this point on, Eve remains *hawwa,* the

xv

archetypal woman and mother and repository of wisdom. As she tells the girls of Plymouth Prep School—millennia later and toward the end of her "autobiography"—"Try being Eve, the first woman, the world / your world," and when they ask her why, she says, "Because you are *Hawwa's* daughters, / and I am."

New. Fresh. Different. And "ne'er so well expressed."

Colquitt's history of the world is the obverse of the universe seen by the church fathers. The myths we grew up with, myths developed over the past four thousand years, were sung and told and written by Jewish, Christian, and Muslim "fathers." Men. The stronger and more dominant sex. Except for the Virgin Mary—and the shadowy unvirgin Eve—women have had no central roles in the myths that dominate our world. And Mary is a late, non-scriptural figure in only one segment of the Judeo-Christian-Islamic mythology. Her veneration, almost completely a Catholic phenomenon, began during the early Middle Ages. In the Bible, she is a vessel for the transporting of God's son from the heavens to the earth. Even Jesus has little to say to her or about her. Woman has always been "the weaker vessel" of the Judeo-Christian-Muslim mythology. (Remember Paul's letter to Timothy: "I permit no woman to teach or have authority over men; she is to keep silent. For Adam was formed first, then Eve; and Adam was not deceived, but the woman was deceived and became a transgressor.") Eve was the easily seduced weaker partner in the Garden of Eden. Her weakness is what caused Adam to be the greater sinner. It was his responsibility to look after himself as well as Eve— weaker physically and intellectually and morally. Despite all we have learned about what Ashley Montague calls "the natural superiority of woman," some theologies still subordinate women to men and make men responsible for teaching wives and daughters "the steep and thorny path to Heaven." After all, a woman preacher, Dr. Johnson says, is like a dog that walks on his hind legs: "It is not done well, but you are surprised to find it done at all."

I think Betsy Colquitt is right when she says that all intelligent people—men and women alike—are feminists. But the feminism that underlies all of Colquitt's work is not the easy, reactive, thoughtless, knee-jerk expostulations that lead to the burning of undergarments and the bashing of males. Hers is a feminism of responsibility. It is the more thoughtful feminism that realizes that women are equal—if not always in stature—certainly in wisdom and in the sight of God. It is a feminism that puts the responsibility for moral and ethical action on both sexes alike. It admits the possibility that women and men are equal in their wrong-doings, that great crimes are as possible at the hands of women as of men. That neither sex has a corner on justice or mercy or revenge or undistilled evil.

The old shibboleths that women are passionate, unreasoning, reacting, tender, and un-responsible will not hold up in the world as defined by Betsy Colquitt. From the Garden of Eden to the Middle Ages and the veneration of Mary to a present where wars are fought to defend "womanhood," we have accepted patriarchal dogma. Colquitt will do no such thing. Her poems all begin with the idea that all ideas, all clichés, all saws and maxims "would be scanned." And scan them she does in the three parts of the present volume—"Eve—from the Autobiography," "Honor Card," and "Uncollected and New Poems."

The Eve poems are divided into two parts; the first part, "garden," traces Eve's thoughts from her awakening in the Garden of Eden, through her discoveries of creatures, language, and implements to her finding Adam, to her meeting the snake—also a "she"—to the sudden changes in the Garden and the ultimate abandonment of the Garden for the larger world. In the second section of the *Eve* poems—"History"—we follow Eve down the ages as she comments from her unique feminine—and feminist—perspectives on the world as it developed after "the Fall"—if indeed it was a "Fall" and not the evolution of all life as seen in one immortal woman's life.

The Eve story is engrossing because this new and radical world view comes to us through eyes and voice unused before by writers and thinkers. The fifty-seven poems in *Eve* form a long continuous narrative spoken by a woman—

actually *Woman*—moving from awakening awareness to calm acceptance to world-worn wisdom. The best way to think of "Eve—from the Autobiography" is as a novel/poem that develops as the character Eve develops. And as Eve grows in knowledge and wisdom, the language of the poems moves from simple to sophisticated. Catching the reader almost unaware, we hear the voice of Eve move from the staccato utterances of the early poems—

> and rushing to grow, meander,
> the honeysuckle, its scents,
> flowers fattening bees, the honey
> vining now from crowded combs
>
> time is present, only, always.
> i know no tenses, nothing
> but the constancy of flowers, . . .("day scene")

to these lines from "Perspective" near the end of the second part of "Eve"

> Then suppose Whitehead's interwoven perspective is
> true, that nothing is independent and symmetry
> of the law of cause/effect is law more than theory—
>
> then past, present, and future bind
> almost to Ptolemy's harmonics,
> and nothing is ever singular, alone
> and nothing is ever lost.

Not only are the ideas in Eve's head simple in her early life and complex four thousand or so years later, her language—Colquitt's language, we must remember—develops similarly. This is one of the glories of Betsy Colquitt's "Eve—from the Autobiography," and it is certainly apparent in all her poems: style and tone and voice follow story and theme. Only true poets accomplish that marriage.

The second part of *Eve* is titled "History." The twenty-four poems in this section comprise Eve's reflections on life from the Garden of Eden near the Tigris-Euphrates Valley to the Big Bend of the Rio Grande Valley—the final poems are "Kafka at Santa Elena" and "In the Big Bend—20th cent. CE." The second poem in the second part of *Eve*, "Entering History," opens—

> I begin again but not as in the beginning.
> Far now from Eden, I enter history,. . .

Eve begins by a recapitulation of her history ("herstory"?) and then says

> I come to understand my role as instrument
> for keeping, change, the woman's part to be,
> act, join past to recurring presents.
> Entering history I begin this journey.

Slowly, it becomes clear that Eve is the spokeswoman for all of us—not just women but men also. It is she who is charged with telling mankind's long trek from the paradise of the First Garden to the present-day valley of the Rio Grande, a garden still unspoiled, still new to the long history of mankind. But suddenly we know that one time is all time, that we live in a world of "recurring presents." In "Letter to Cain," she says, "I would like to know how your city / planning goes, when the mall opens" and then tells him

> Your father ages, talks sometimes
> of trying for social security.
> Perhaps we'll leave this land,
> move to Babel.

The juxtaposing of past and present echoes modernist poets like Eliot (cf. "Unreal City" in *The Waste Land)* who shift time backwards and forwards without comment. In "Eve" we see Cain, doomed to wander, live in a world of city planning and malls. Adam considers social security. And haven't we all moved to Babel, the fabled city of noise and incommunication? But biblical time passes, and in "Separations" she grieves for the death of Adam, for "Abel long buried." For Cain and Seth and all who grow old. All except Eve, who lives in what Keats calls "slow time"—

> I know myself *hawwa, the living one*
> schooled by Eden, to learn by other pasts,
> to live in many presents,
> each past, each present, rich
> in loss, hurt, wonder, marvel.

Then down the centuries Eve observes and participates in the circling years and centuries. She visits Machiavelli, answers a query from *Who's Who*, visits Emily Dickinson in "Alias Mrs. Adam." (Dickinson, in a letter reprinted as epigraph, calls herself "Mrs. Adam," mentions that there is no record of Eve's death in the Bible, and asks "and why am I not Eve?" Of course she is; we all are.) Eve watches Schliemann dig, sees Freud, Kafka, St. Francis, joins the lecture circuit to visit the girls at Plymouth Prep, and once remembers Adam while she is at a supermarket, sees him mirrored in an old man "Once easy in homespuns, he stifles now / in double knit of polyester, / this old man fashioned far from garden. . . . "

So Eve moves eternally through the world of slow time— doing, observing, reflecting, teaching, being. In our "fast time," she rests at Santa Elena Canyon:

> I home here, journey when I please,
> am needed, receive many visitors,
> plan to stay, the long ago garden I seek
> in time, story, change, in self, selves—
> > wholeness never complete—
> always to seek, try to make,
> perhaps to be again in this place
> where I am, have my kiva,
> this Santa Elena where I am
> begin again and again.

Always seeking, always *Hawwa*, always Woman.

Besides the "Eve" poems, the present collection reprints *Honor Card* (1980), a collection of forty-two poems arranged in four parts, as well as fifty-five uncollected or hitherto unpublished poems—this third section divided into five parts. The subjects range across art, literature, travel, marriage, domesticity, nature, and religio-philosophical speculation. The poems in the two final sections are not as person-centered as the "Eve" poems, but then since all poems are filtered through a personality, it is perhaps more accurate to say that Colquitt's filterings in these final two segments are impersonally personal. There is none of the confessional whine that mars some Romantic—and much immature modern—poetry; no "I fall upon the thorns of life, I bleed." Even when we sense that Colquitt is commenting on things close to her—marriage and family, for instance—she maintains a distance from the personal. Despite the number of marriage poems in the second and third sections of the present volume, all reflecting Colquitt's conviction that marriage is a form of unarmed combat, the distance is such that we can never be sure that the marriages in question represent her own experience—though it would be hard to conclude otherwise. The first of the marriage poems in the *Honor Card* section will serve as an example of Colquitt's restraint. In "The Lie and Truth of This Land," a poem that uses the images of "wars and alarums" to signify the vicissitudes of married life, we see a couple embarking upon a marriage—or a marital campaign:

> Bonded, trothed, we foraged separately,
> each army wanting provender and uncomfortable
> in bivouac.

But time passes, skirmishes are fought, and by the end of the poem there is a peace—however temporary:

> our armies mainly easy at armistice
> and rarely foraging, commissaried now
> mostly from home.

As many of her other marital poems show, the circling "left and right through cul-de-sacs" that is marriage is never easy. As Colquitt has pointed out, "marital" and "martial" are matters of reversed letters only.

Too much explication may destroy the pleasures of the reader, who will certainly want to savor the poems without the intercessory ramblings of an introduction writer, but it is hard not to keep pointing out the small miracles that Betsy Colquitt has wrought. There are the delightful poems celebrating the lives and deaths of Cummings, Frost, Eliot, and William Carlos Williams in the five sections entitled "of some recent dead" in *Honor Card*. The poems mimic and play off the most famous lines of the dead poets; here is one:

> how do you Mister Death
> like e. e.
> cummings at you
>
> coming with lyrics and love into
> your really enormous room
> coming wide-eyed and word handsome. . . .

Cummings captured perfectly: the tortured syntax, the wide-eyed blue-eyed puddlewonderful language that marks this most romantic of modern American poets.

One has only to compare the wit and frivolity of "of some recent dead" with another poem in *Honor Card* to see Colquitt's range. The elegy "For Frank, Lost in the China Sea" compares the young man's death with Icarus falling into the sea off Crete and, in tranquility, remembers the man:

> Now in Texas season
> gaudy with Judas,
> orchards in flame,
> pears in communion dress,
> I hear of that plunging moment
> and would speak his Icarian
> unlegended descent
> sharpening in blunt words
> feeling not of kin-grief
> but keen at loss of him
> once student, then pilot and dead.

Even the half-dozen or so famous elegies in English hardly surpass this memorial to Frank "once student, then pilot and dead." Colquitt's poem has dignity and sharpness of observation and restraint. In this poem, as in all Colquitt's poetry, the overflow of emotions is always recollected in—if not tranquility—at least in distance and controlled passion.

Even in the final poem in this volume, "Return," which I take to be occasioned by the sudden death in 1991 of Landon Colquitt, the writer's husband, the restraint is complete though the reader can hardly hold back the tears. In the poem the speaker addresses the dead man as she imagines (dreams) him suddenly home. She tells him that if he returned, she, "surprised, glad,/would hold you like life,/warm your hands, feet, cold body" and then

> after you supped and I fed
> on the marvel of your presence,
> you'd tell me how it was
> your sudden leaving,
> how you called—think you did—my name
> but I didn't answer. So swift it was,
> the way things go with the heart.

After he has told her where he had been, "news of this strange place," they would dream

> you that you were home
> I that your dream was true.

As is the case with all Betsy Colquitt's poems, the language of "Return" is new and fresh and sometimes startling. It performs what Conrad says is the artist's role—"Above all to make you see." The style is modern (to call it modernist or postmodern is to use terms "too often profaned") in that Colquitt proceeds as often by indirection as by direction—the topic is often only suggested by the analogue. In "non-pro," the speaker at "three and fifty" sees life in terms of football; three and ten (third and ten yards to go) is optimistic,

> but three and fifty's no metaphor
> in this real, undaylight saving—
>
> clock ticking, odds rushing
> to dark as time runs down
> to the two-minute warning,
> the final time out.

In this poem, as in all the others in the collection, the language is clipped and taut, catching the tempo of fleeting life that modern man—"Yea, and woman, too"—bemoans. The finality. The uncertainty. The "withdrawing roar" of Arnold's Sea of Faith. In such a world, the cryptic must pass for commentary; if life's rhyme and reason are obscure, the soft rhymes and rhythms of poetry seem out of date. The new poetry must be as harsh and disjointed as our thoughts—or at least seem to be. And capital letters must be husbanded for use.

In poem after poem—far too many to explicate in the space allotted to an introduction writer—Betsy Colquitt sums up the world she has lived in (and brightened) for seventy years. Long after most poets have used up what the Anglo-Saxons called their "word-hoard," Betsy Colquitt is still finding new ways to make us see. Many of the poems in this volume—almost all of the *Eve* poems and many of those in "Uncollected and New Poems"—are new within the past decade. And she continues to write. Her career defies the cliché that poets burn themselves out early. It's true that Coleridge and Wordsworth, though they lived to be old, lost the "the visionary gleam" and the "inner joy" before age forty. And Byron and Shelley and Keats—Dorothy Parker's "trio of lyrical treats"—died young. But Frost and Yeats maintained the spark almost to the end. Sophocles was writing *Oedipus at Colonus* at ninety. And Betsy Colquitt gave birth to Eve long after many have retired to Highgate.

A proper introduction to a writer should begin with a biographical sketch, but I have saved the exterior facts of Betsy Colquitt's life for last because her poetry comes so much from an inner, unsummarizable life that biography seems an afterthought. I can think of few writers whose work appears so little influenced by surroundings, even though a number of the poems in this collection center on Fort Worth and a few of them speak of home and family. Still, Colquitt has so refined her experiences that each piece takes on its own life—a life strangely apart from the writer. But duty calls, so here are some biographical data. Born

Betsy Feagan in a house on Berry Street almost within sight and sound of Texas Christian University in Fort Worth, Colquitt has spent almost all of her seventy years in the shadow of TCU. After taking her BA (magna cum laude) at TCU in 1947, she studied for the MA (1948) at Vanderbilt University, which still had about it the aura of Robert Penn Warren, Allen Tate, and that band of agrarian poets, novelists, and critics who had decamped a few years earlier. Between 1948 and 1954, she taught at the University of Alabama at Montevallo, the University of Kansas, and the University of Wisconsin. In 1954, she married Landon Colquitt and joined the English faculty at TCU where her husband was a mathematics professor.

During her years (1954-1995) on the TCU faculty, Betsy Colquitt published scores of poems, books, scholarly articles, and reviews—while finding time to be mother to two daughters, one a physician in Texas, the other a professor of English in California. Despite not having taken the PhD, usually a requirement for senior rank, Colquitt became a full professor in her department and was the first recipient, in 1982, of the Chancellor's Award for Distinguished Teaching. For almost thirty years, she was editor of *Descant*, one of the state's most respected literary journals. Her work as writer, teacher, and editor earned her grants from the Frost Foundation and the Texas Commission on the Arts and the recognition of being listed in *Contemporary Authors, Who's Who of American Women, Directory of American Scholars, and World Who's Who of Women*.

The best way to summarize Betsy Colquitt's influence on her world may be to quote from one of her most popular poems—"poetry and post, texas." In the poem, the speaker, obviously judging a high school poetry contest, comes across a West Texas boy with "the gift":

> he's never seen a daffodil
> nor does Pecos flow like Avon,
> yet this marvelous boy manned of language
> visions his landscape whole

. . . .
it's not enough to judge he's won:
he's by God a poet, and Post
and all West Texas
can never be proclaimed again
the same.

Betsy Colquitt has made a difference, and those of us who read her "can never be proclaimed again the same."

Eve
from
the
Autobiography

garden

i wake to the garden,
to its being, to my being,
know i am, and begin
to name this world.

walking amid grasses
i enjoy many gifts. i hear
papyrus reed breeze,
winds lyre these i call trees,
a mangrove, cypress, the plane,
willows swaying by waters.

i discover the sun
and my sister the moon
and the constellations—
    the big dipper—i say.
eying berenice's hair
i strand it to heavenly order.

breeze touches me
and i joy in olive-scented air
in which i am
and am not, bound too
to winsome earth.

i fill air with my namings,
wonder of sparrow, majesty
of hawk, marvel of butterfly,
    its soul-rich grace.

others easy in water
dart, hide, play as they swim,
their scales iridescent,
a spectrum i stroke
as i teach them tameness.

walking in water, i call my dolphin
who comes, rubs my legs, schools me
in touch. i scratch the spiny shark
and listen to music of whales.

sheep and my dog companion me
easily, naturally. lion in coat
of many shades is shy,
but elephant, wily with lithe proboscis,
trumpets from savanna at my call.

i name and invent the horse.
eohippus, i say to her
delighting in hoofs, motion
as centaured we speed by her strength.

i study the lively ground,
my keen eyes sighting ants, worms,
chipmunks, rabbits,
the prairie dogs unburrowed.

made, named, these and more
know themselves, their wills,
and the world fills with life, lives
as i fill with mine.

i pleasure in being, these beings
as i am, one amid many,
this plenty as i name,
make as word this new world.

am-ing

alert, rapt to learn this world,
i name it copiously: this, no more,
and everything.
in this beginning of word, words,
i abstract to sign with sounds my world,
its many beings, lives, my self
one of these but different as witness
from lion, lamb, wildebeest,
each in tune with nature, their natures
but not by words though they speak
in many ways, by motions, scents,
sounds unlike my syllables.

different too from trees
flourishing, busy with their rustling
that do not name themselves *fig, baobab,*
their parts *root, leaf, fruit.*

different from the river dumb
to word its melody of sweet waters
and from briny gulf mute
to taste its salt as name or tell
its liquidity, motion, destination.

in this place of beginnings
i only word, observe to name,
know self as vocabulary,
and i please in this making
and see it is good.

keen to learn—and i do—
i discover weaving when i divide
my long hair in heavy strands,
braid it to supple rope.
walking by river, seeing my image
ripple, *eve,* i say, *hawwa,*
the living one, and i am.

day scene

in this prime spring
season stays in stasis,
the ground a crazy quilt
of winecups, daffodils,
bluebonnets, larkspurs,

low banks of the wadis
trooping with colors,
lupins bringing sky to earth,
indian paintbrush drawing
reds, yellows to petals,
hedges of wildroses
swathed in pink.

the trees abloom,
dogwood, peach,
palm, orange, olive, mimosa,
mesquite,

and rushing to grow, meander,
the honeysuckle, its scents,
flowers fattening bees, the honey
vining now from crowded combs.

time is present, only, always.
i know no tenses, nothing
but the constancy of flowers,
their perfumes, colors in what
i call *now,* am in and of
and can name.

i pleasure in this now,
this *primavera,* its beauty,
in my names and will make
more words and something
different, other than words.

the basket case

i can weave a case for this,
the winds waving supple grasses
willing to bind as my hair
to strand to order, holding.

braiding this afternoon
i've no penelope thoughts,
no plan beyond the technomorphic,
imagine green grasses, tans, grays
joining to new patterns,

nor do i work like atlas.
world i carry is light, easy,
and i am light years from work
as form emerges from grasses
bonding, their leaves binding
to this that can hold more fruits
than my hands can carry.

made by my nature's making,
this container waits to contain,
does, and will—this i call *basket,*

and i find this new making
different from naming
and as rich in prospects.

i learn to do, to be by action,
inevitable this discovery
once i see, admire grasses
lacing, learn to braid hair
lush but breeze-worried
when i walk, ride.

i can make a case for this,
freely will, for the natural
nature of this creation
granted my being, naming,
garden's burgeoning,
grasses weaving as they do, must,
my self making as woman does, must.

learning to think in elephants

sylvia i say to my cat
come from dense woods.
george i say to my dog,
who follows me gardening.
clement i say to my dove
at home in live oak's arms.

but as i say their names
i know my syllables label
particulars of this variorum,
sylvia, george, clement
nominals in this my eden, my delight
where i also need to word plurals.

i learn to think in elephants,
mine as one among similars,
my giraffe as kin to kind,
my green monkey as sister
to others of her verdant shape,
wildebeest herding with his likes,
baobab standing in lexical grove.

once this perception,
grammar follows
naturally, unnaturally,
and i search for verbs
energetic to act, eager to be.

then i can sentence, dance to ideas,
distract my self with abstraction,
can fashion the true and not known.

i want joiners, find
conjunctions, prepositions
to clarify my propositions.

achieving my language,
my speech structures
to subtle, and eden is no more
the same nor i, for i speak, tell
like none else, shape eden, this place
of delight, by my sentences.

night scene 1

order architects first to the doric
but in bounty
garden tends to baroque
as each day births the prodigal.

my home, this kiva, its shape
drawn from my basket,
opens to moon, stars, the pleiades,
admits harmonies as heaven choirs
in its night beauty, the lights,
sounds of skyfolk in their orbits
singing glad songs in, of space

while earth dark now and easy
is quiet and at rest.

wifery

the world is mine to keep
and i keep it as i can.
i watch, learn from nature
to protect, to direct nature
to model of its self.

nothing espaliers, but as all grow
at will, at their pleasure,
garden jungles, and i seek
to keep order amid burgeoning
in these first days of this real estate.

but as i move, remove grasses,
shape, tie trees to their self-interest,
twine blackberries to mine,
my hands, arms, legs thorn-wounded,

i learn the limits of many constants—
busyness grows me no new fingers.
of necessity i rely on wit to mother
this world, devise the idea of *tools*,
and assay stones to hone,
polish to an edge that cuts.

daily i see, learn how constant
the wifery to keep, tend this world,
this primer of garden new
to its being as i am new to mine,
and i seek to understand this other,
these many others, and my self.

handing clay

in mid-morning heat
my fingers find cool in clay

moist, pliant at my touch.
as my palms round clay to ball,

i think of form, of a shape
like the nest where cardinals home.

my useful thumb indents,
smooths, soothes this soil

to a pleasing miniature
of that which i know, love.

i think *pots*, ponder their uses,
but busy with garden, i abandon clay.

return at dusk to find clay sun-changed,
and i wonder on the uses of warmth.

when weeds collect
and i gather them to piles,

heat hides in these heaps,
these once-green brown

metamorphosing to mulch.
when night brings its chill,

i remember these dead greens
razing to embers that warm.

i occupy myself with leaves, sticks,
flint, other promethean things,
and this occupation catches *fire*.

garden keeping

i watch over garden,
follow its changes,

when flowers lose blooms, color,
grasses brown and seed,

see those born to water grow
in time's transforming,

tree limbs take on new shapes
that grate, bruise one another,

hedges become rife, sprawling—
these changes alter
and world changes from itself.

only by my doing
can this place stay in health,
keep its first loveliness.
i learn the word *work*,
and by my work,
beauty begins its return.

i trim, pull at grasses,
spread thick ground cover
to bare space,
lead animals to farther pastures,
birds to more distant trees,
lure the trusting to pristine streams.

to keep garden as its self
requires change, my changes
else first splendor, wonder
of this home falls to wild,

to disorder betraying its reality,
the marvel of the beginning,
of change and of many beginnings.

oneness

through the day
i note pairing.

walking by night,
i think *comfort*
seeing those resting
together in warmth.

i learn my oneness
in world that speaks

of union, lasting
or brief, and of bearing.

i think of one kin to my kind,
of woman making another

akin to her self, this being
i might fashion, bring forth.

psalm

You guide me
as i guide my sheep,
and i know no want.

You lead me to rest
in greenest pastures
safe beside the still waters,
and restore my soul.

You show me paths
to the good, the right,
and to the world alive
with lives, beings, this world
i know, name, tend, cherish.

should my path lead
through dark valleys,
i will fear no danger,
no harm as You,
Holy Lady,
        my comfort, my companion
guide me to light.

You prepare for me, give me
this place rich in beauty,
wonders. You anoint me
with sweet-scented oils.
by Your grace, my being,
my grace lives, flourishes.

surely Your goodness and mercy
will attend me all my days
as i dwell always, forever at home
in Your holiness, with You,
my Holy Lady, my loving God.

inventing the wheel

these days growth springs
every where. from rocky seed,
a shoot births, brownest stick
banners with flowers, leaves.

fell remains want tending
as hillocks of moldering gather,
and i basket heaps
with these leavings,

think to frame as compost
these fertile embers
and i act, move, remove,
back willing and pliant

to bend, gather, order
this first spring.
i begin to think in engineering,
how much to move,

how sized this basket,
how larger container
moved not only by my back
might aid and many-hand me.

i think form, forms, and contrive
from shape of leaf, pine cone,
model of apple, but none
conforms to my need.

pondering apple, i wonder
on its roundness sectioned,
cut this fruit with my honed rock,
and this slice of apple shapes

to circle that rolls willingly
on my hand, over ground,
even a hill. this fruitful
contrivance a model

for tool sturdier than fruit
and able to cart biggest
baskets and their fill.
this invention i call *wheel,*
and i see this making is good.

the keeping of words

i make, say words, name this world,
its many lives, ways of being—
trees and other greening things,
animals, fish, birds, waters,
the sky, its clouds, living lights.

as i say words, i keep them
in what i name *mind*, return to them
in *thought*. but spoken they vanish,
leave no mark on lips, earth, air
though animals, fish too at times,

who speak but make no words,
know the sounds that are their names
and respond to my calls.
thinking how I know travel
of the lion by his paw prints,

birds by feathers lost in flight,
grasses, plants by leaf signs,
i wish my best creation to translate
to signs more durable than only sound.
i think of syllables as visible,

feather for bird, four toes for sloth,
light lines to be star, a large round
for sun, lines as rays, a small round
for the many-faced moon,
and to symbol myself, an oval for head,

three lines braiding for hair, other lines,
longer, more graceful for body, all these
to sign the outward *eve*, like my baskets
containing more than a sign can show.
i try marking rock with other rocks

that grind to no scratch, their hardness
unyielding. i try marks with shale,
its brittle, soft lines lost to first dew.
i think of poke bush, its red berries
staining my hands reaching for greens.

as i squeeze these berries, my hands dye
purple as grapes. dipping a reed in this juice,
i make marks, draw on rock's smooth surface.
as i limn this place, i give words

another language. i think of word
for this language distinct
from nature's signs and more lasting.
i name this act *scribing*,
its symbol, a hand holding reed.

pots

sun-hard, ready now to hold ink,
berries, grains, fruits, wines,
to nurture young plants in their growing,
these pots have many shapes
crafted to best use, crafty too to eye.

garden now wears many colors,
and i wish to color my terra cottas
to hues like grasses, shades subtle
as roses, bright like night skies,
blues evoking the waters sunning.

from the variegate hues of umber, ochers,
vermilion, berries, white lime, soot,
lapis lazuli abundant as sky,
i press, grind, bond dyes with fats,
water, yolk, tie hairs to reed for brush,
pluck a goose feather for quill,
and try color on clay.

my colors make signs, cross-hatches, grids,
herringbone like geese in flight, my strokes
imitating what i see, know, the plants,
shells, fishes of this place, and image too
the being i know, worship but do not see.

my pots painted, drying, i think
of colors on swells of cave rock
where paints might show the bison,
horses, a cow, even the unicorn
i saw today unfenced and uneasy,

and think of my kiva, its adobe
adorned with many-colored flowers,
shells, and signs that have meanings.
wonder too on that that pleases,
this new beauty kin to nature
but different, other than the beauty

of nature, of that i know in sound
of words, sounds i make with reeds,
gourds, wood hollowed and covered.
i please in these new languages,
this artless, playful pleasure
of making the new in this new world.

adam

warm in warmth of afternoon
i linger in brief shelter of plane,
my hand cooled by the clay,
its sources for invention,
its roots for making not all known.

suddenly this strange soil breeding
scarabs quickens, gives
as finger comes forth and i take it,
hand, arm coming free of burying earth

and bound to that i must heave
to air, life, and i do.

he is clay-coated and ugly,
his strange umbilical linked still
to his source. unwife
i discover midwifery.

with my hands i knife him free,
unmud his fair skin,
unseal his shut eyes,
and bind up his wounds with my troth.

i touch him awake and he wakens,
he listens as i speak him our names,
inform him our geography
prepared by my hands as our world.

of its many tongues i teach him
my language, *ādām* i say, *man,*
and we only know our only names,
one another, and of ourselves
will make our own kind.

bowering 1

sweet as olive scent,
gentle as dolphin's touch,
kindly tongued as doves,
we feast, hunger for other
and of our otherness make
this new one out of two,
this bower rich, richer
than garden, playful, artful
beyond my signs,
and lively by night, by day.

joined we find new vocation,
this *marriage* we name it,
this bower, my kiva, our sanctuary
for our selves, our union
blessed by the presence
of the Lady smiling
on our joy as we explore
human, humane worlds
to learn this new language,
new speech by day, by night.

of holy days

sentenced to think, i think *past*
and probe *memory*, which ripens
with words, reconstructs
by sounds, signs garden mornings
of first words when being
and naming for me were all,
when there were no seasons
and i did not conjugate,
need to make tenses.

to speak of first days as holy,
blessed, full only of wonder is true,
but later days too whole to holiness
in us two who are one
and marvel on this new being,
our new languages, and makings
of other and many kinds.

lacking the pentecost
of my lavish tongue tasting words,
i could not tell of this timely place,
its varying days, vanished seasons
still alive by language
when lush grapes are raisins
and trees once lush branch bare,

nor unworded could i preserve
my self, presence that i was,
or this time with adam as companion.

in time to come, my words will tell
my, our story, be grist for scribes
eager to claim, homestead
this once-place far from them,
perhaps to obscure my story,

turn it to theirs, these decipherers
interpreting my text by an alien schooling,
education in patristic tools.

to things a season

green, grapes hide,
heavy vines twining
through tallest trees.
we watch, the birds and i,
as bunches ripen,
fill with sweetness
heavy with purpleness.

then the birds come,
feast on grapes
yet hunger.

i feast too on this plenty,
these succulents
once hard, their juice
scouring my tongue with acid.

change abounds in this place
where all grows, matures,
antlers shed to be reborn,
furs thinning, thickening,
pale cardinals turning scarlet,
snakes renewing, old skins left
like strange leaves;
in rise, fall of river, sea moving
to tides; in sun, moon, stars
that guard the days, the nights
varying in durations, heaven's bodies
moving to new places, powers
as seasons alter, change
from prime of beginning
when garden was constant and delight.

eating these ripe grapes, i think
of change in this world's way,
perceive *time* as idea, and think
the same eve cannot step twice
into the same river.
in summer's late heat,
i see the river from which
all rivers flow is a summer river
stingy with its waters.

looking at my face wrinkling
in this river's sandy bed, i know
my self living in a world loosed
to seasons with change as its constant.

i wonder on snake shedding old skin,
ponder renewal, find more questions
than my language answers.
i turn interrogative, ask and ask,
feast on grapes and hunger
for that i can't name.

night scene 2

the sleep of things is short,
and more than heaven wakes
these nights when doric
falls to the baroque.

i know this change
one comet-troubled night
when silence turns restive
with night-beings prowling
as is their night nature,
watch rodents plunder grain,
armadillos hunt, sloth rouse to prey,
hear lions fight over kill.

by day growth rampants,
the garden a wilderness now
for my hands, my tools to keep.
maguey thorns, kudzu wildfires,
trumpet vines bury the ground-bound—
cucumbers, melons, mosses.

i learn about wanting help,
my own night nature prowling
new domains, a hunter stalking
beyond day limits.

bowering 2

he sleeps heavily, our long day
keeping, weeding, bowery dalliance
falling upon him as he rests
dreaming his own visions

while i lie restless in bower
once comfort, home to pleasure,
but now a shelter unsheltering,
the safe in danger as nights bring
lions close, hyenas to near rocks,
vines lively in dark as in light
tendril to enclose—honeysuckle
tying its knots, kudzu leaping
to prison us some morning.

more and more, i, he must act,
work to stay as we can
the garden raging to wildness,
must guard order for the life
of nature, its being, many beings,
and for other and self.

i school in meaning
of troth plighted, my flesh welded
to other as my own, but not proud
this flesh nor desperate,
sufficient self still.

wedded, i remain monogamous
but single, separate as the dove
nesting with her mate
as she dreams her own dreams,
as the cattle herding for warmth
feel single cold, single warmth.

awake, sleeping adam wakes
to his own, his solitary being,
and the language of his sleep
is his own tongue.
when he sounds from dream
lilith, lilith,
i hear, dumb to his lexicon.

wheel reconsidered

i know my self partial,
piece in the puzzle
of wholeness that is creation,

a being among many beings,
all moving, changing, these
the only constants and ceaseless,
and i wish wholeness.

i invent, use my pristine head
to extend my limits—
        sic non es vocatus
        fac te vocatum—
someone later will say.
not vocated to wholeness
but called to its yearning,
i try by extension
to fashion a whole-some world.

sadly i invent the wheel,
invention not easy like basket
or pots birthed by nature's ways.
with wheel i try many shapes
wrong from nature, in nature.
then from my mind,
i shape that which is *wheel*,
its roundness apt for movement,
its strength greater than mine,
this tool designed to cope
with abundance flooding garden,

and am left in this brown study,
to invent, reinvent forever this self,
its extensions, and to probe
its meanings, seek, find and not.

god mothering

but with all my making
i make and do not make
my self, my world.

am comforted by the presence
of this other akin and not
to my self and like nothing else
in this place and beyond.

this presence does not speak
my language but Hers
unworded but heard, this presence
of Her who is unseen, who is love
and gives me being, lets me create,
discover, make meanings.

i sense Her nearness in mute footfall,
the sound of one hand clapping,
feelings, sensations i have
in the daily of that
which is more than the daily.

i glimpse mystery that forms,
informs the garden, the world
and us in it.

when i sense presence in absence,
in hiding, i phrase no paradox
but very statement, and i await
revelation as i feel awe
at this presence i honor
in my practice of, in the daily.

i offer no fruit, blood gifts
to this presence, but standing
at morning by the rain tree gilded
with blooms, i envision an altar
and would worship there,
offering my self, being, work,
love to this creator, creation
nurturing life in its coming to be.

the sky does not comment

is silent now. if once i heard
music from its turning lights,

what the sky sings now is shy, sly,
inaudible though order, the random

exist in this space of limitless dark
obscure in origins, its nature a rune

and mysterious like earth, the springs
erupting now everywhere in eden

that could overpower the garden,
flood it, drown it with their plenty.

the constellations, my calendar,
tell me when to plant, expect to reap,

store against bare seasons,
but order of sky gives me a meager map

spread across vastness beyond my acres,
hectares, and distant this space,

innocent of earth changes, of the springs,
their gifts if they are, their destructions.

and what of these dog days I wonder.
heat fierce, desert strangely humid

as sky hurls perseids earthward
as shards. i wish harmony,

music from a geometer's model
of order, but my wishes make no song.

the only music i hear is atonal
and is deaf to harmony.

night scene 3

sylvia discovers the uses of claws
and i discover scratches.
george tires of grains, learns of prey,
and i see his canines redden.

blood diets the hawk finding
the power of beak to beckon
rabbit from brushy hiding,
and luring song of mockingbird

calls to moth and monarch.
i shock and not at this predation,
world as it is in its youth
in this creation full of wills

where harmony thrives with
violence born by those who prey
and borne by those born to be prey
to hunters skilled and awkward.

weaponed now, i am cunning
with words, stones, knives.
lacking claws, beaks, real canines,
i devise their similars, my extensions
the night music sounding in day

as my song turns mime
of this world benign
and dangerous, a siren song
beckoning with consonance
that belies dissonance, danger.

ninth month

his brief act is enough
i am so nearly parthenogenetic,
my body fecund as garden
and lithe, healthy, young.

i create what our union made,
and this quickening creation
brings my flesh to fleshly focus.

observant, i know by others
        heifer, doe, elephant, my cat
this littering condition,
unwieldy, cumbersome,
this i carry growing
unknown, unobserved.

moving dinosaur-heavy,
i long to be light,
yearn this birth,
but this guest in my body
moves to its rhythm, time.

fat and flesh-swollen
i wait, my body thistly,
grotesque as it creates another
separate, single like its makers,
and eager to assert itself,
its own powerful will.

eden at supper

i observe, watch waters
as swift fish dart to feed,
lusting to taste their own kind,
watch owl wake at evening,

scan field for smallest mouse,
wing to talon this catch
hiding itself in weeds.
then mouse becomes shape it isn't

when, unsuited to flight, it flies,
beak taking it far from ground.
lion, teethed for other than grasses,
seeks gazelle, cattle, and more

as diet. i can reckon
that these torn to nurture others
are made to be hurt, eaten
and that their destiny too

is cortex dulled to pain,
but air-borne, mouse screams;
pursued, fish hide, try to;
and gazelle's cortex

cries in fear at coming pain.
when I unhead grains, gather fruits,
i think nature does not shudder,
nor does it in these kills

for meat, for blood to sup,
nature, this world
with its loveliness, terror,
inexorable wills, instincts

other than i'd will them,
other than i'd will mine.

thinking autochthonous

i think *origins*, ponder how being
began, how it comes.
knowing adam's birth
and thinking autochthonous,
i toy with earth, form homunculus
which never breathes, comes alive.

clay easily gives life to pots, jars,
forms that in gopher wood
will craft to ark,
that in bricks will make dwellings
to shelter many.
clay forms easily to designs—arc, circle, triangle,
a pentagon like a star—
that hold promise, might be,
become signs of the holy,
the Lady formless but present.

but not again
does clay as such
birth a new life.

ignorant of origins,
unknowing of mine,
i design forms to make
signs of that which i see
and of that i can't know.

had i a genealogy,
genealogy would not suffice
since ancestry must trace
to the first mothering.
had i story beyond that i know,
an ur-text i lack, to label
neanderthal or *cro-magnon*
would evade my question.

i find no other like myself
nor does spirit i feel tell me
my source, but when the Lady
is near, i no longer question,
no longer feel absence
as my companion, forget
to ask, to look for answers.

gorgoning

a stony day, granite as the heart,
i look at what to do
        acres of henbit to hoe
        hectares of grain ready to reap
        ripe, overripe blackberries
        to pick from prickly stems—
and tire in prospect of this labor.

walking toward the field of grain,
i've no banter for george
        content in his work as friend,
don't pat his head, snatch my hand
away from his grainy tongue,
offer no praise for his dashes, returns,
speak only to command.

sickling the full-headed grasses
i'm unyielding as granite,
scythe swiftly beheading,
scaring rabbits fearing mayhem.

home near dark, i speak no greeting,
speak hardly at all, heavy now,
gargantuan outward and inward.

while last sun haggles with clouds,
i haggle too, injure
with a fencer's fierce courtesy,
and bedded, seem to sleep but lie.

posed at rest, i salute the gorgon
stoning in my heart, invent
this inventive condition
distant from my other inventions.

in teeming world, teeming body,
i learn of a new meaning of oneness,
the loneness of being all one.

ringing changes

this new present is filled
with words, baskets, many tools,
with skill in fire, cookery,
music, drawings on kiva
inside and out, horses parade in cave,

and garden is put to our use,
which alters garden, us
as garden changes by growth
moving to ripeness and to fall.
i cannot of change say
ripeness turns to *fall,*
cannot of change see
our fortune as *happy, sad*
better, worse, am ignorant
of how if unending
first state i knew would be,
can imagine constancy as tedium,
life as lived in a pastoral scene,

but imagination i imagine
constructs its own reality,
tedium thought real
makes this thought reality.

i can imagine first days as being,
only this, no memory needed,
the first always present, constant,
fresh, refreshing, no need for names,
words to be made.

though i could so imagine, i don't,
choose to imagine change as constant,
as altering as destiny and never tedious
even if limits, hurt, loss come to be,
and i, we are, be by becoming.

rite

i wake to cool of dawn,
free myself from leafy cover
to the morning's chill,
sun hidden under gray blankets.

i enact my morning acts,
plan our day in this shadowed garden,
walk to the tree always green, bearing fruit
where we worship this mystery
of presence and absence.

as i look to tree, i see fronds sway.
adam hears messages in this movement,
i hear breezes and no more.

speak i wish to say but cannot
and do not believe what adam hears
is other than the tree's language,
its leaves blown by breeze,
its branches tethered by green tree snakes
winsome as leaf pods.

languages of eden

always i am articulate
but i listen too, hear
adam's language
and others' too, the dove's
call to mate, to young,
cattle lowing from meadows,
the rooster waking the sun,
my dog's battles, triumphs
speaking from dreams.

when snake speaks,
her speech is no surprise
except by its likeness to mine,
this indo-european snake
whose tongue belongs
to my language group.

resting in afternoon heat
of this late fall,
adam does not hear this talk,
but swollen with child,
uncomfortable now, i sleep little
but walk, listen, hear.

her offer is minor, something
in the way of translation
> offer uninviting
> given my wordgift,
> skill with my language,
> others' languages,
> even serpentine tongues.

untempted, i continue to walk,
heavy, uneasy, secure and not
in this changing world
conversant with many tongues,
all their glosses yet to be made.

search

things go off course. cattle stray
from familiar pastures, sheep on a whim
wander far to graze on imagined greenery.
while i seek to bring them home,
george roams, chases unknown prey,
ignores my call to come back.

from a place my voice can't reach,
i hear his shrill sounds saying *pain.*
i try to follow his sound, beckon him
now beyond hearing any voice.

i miss him displaced from
his, my usual ways, right place.
he teaches me loss, and i learn.

though i search garden,
follow the sun miles beyond it,
i find only desert, the vast sands
with few plants, none i know,
no life i see except mirages
and black birds cawing, diving

as clouds gather, rise fiery as volcanos.
then thunder erases all other sound
save the lightning's, forks stabbing
at sand as rain floods this dry world.

baptized by storm, i enter a new world,
storm filling arroyos, any ditch.
these waters roil, speed
to bury the garden, all lowlands.

but over even the sounds of storm,
rushing waters, i hear calls
of drowning sheep, unhomed cattle,
their fear, pain, and listen
for a call that won't come.

the sodden earth is ice-slick
and i fall, rain hitting my body
like stones. when i can rise,
sun pierces clouds
and water-buried world blazes,
flames like St. Elmo's fire.

epilogue

waters subsided, i return
to my buried garden,
its strange springs stilled.
i find adam. together
we search our world, its ruin
        the bloated carcasses
        of animals we loved, named,
        the unearthed trees,
        broken limbs of the standing,
        blooms washed away,
        my rain tree ungilded,
        locked in a casket of earth.

we discover only wreckage,
explore remains. to catalogue
the watermarked survivors
of our making is quick
        a tree-caught basket
        mud-filled and distended,
        wheelbarrow sinking under load
        of silt the river, rivers brought,
        wheel, knife, chisel entombed
        for others later to unearth.

bower, kiva is hovel,
its adobe now earth again.

but mind remembers bower,
stocks baskets, wheels,
use of reeds, brushes, colors,
is tooled for making, creating,
and has a larger lexicon,
knows words like *disaster, pain,*
death, longing, survival.

all human now and with memory,
we survive as witnesses
to garden's past, its presence
in our past, our future.
ungardened, i am, remain eve, *hawwa.*

i call to adam. as we move
from ruin, i feel quickening,
this birth of self, of adam, of others
faithed to act, remember, hope, love.

part 2

History

Interpreters

"Do you realize, Eve, . . . the curse of God pronounced
on your sex weighs still on the world . . .? The image of
God, Adam, you broke him as if he were a plaything.
You deserved death, and it was Adam who had to die."

—Tertullian

Cranach liked his Eves nubile, Michelangelo
favored the muscled, Masaccio the grieving nude,
van Eyck the pregnant. Milton searched centuries
and Calvinist heart to paint his suppliant Eve
necessary weakness in order father-god forged.

I exist and not
in these depictions. I survive Church fathers,
their celibate dreams, outlast Augustine,
his lust a pain even foregone, renounced.

Paul for all his virgin zeal
conceded marriage the remedy for burning,
and in time, that peculiar institution
becomes sacrament, Adam saint—
not my plaything,
Eden days canonized as *felix culpa.*

Mary's story alters my story, she as mother,
I as first mother; she immaculately conceived,
I unnaveled and, even sternest doctors
acknowledge, of unusual origin.

Most, Mary's story and mine parallel

49

as parables of grief, her son, my sons
dying, my losses graced by no lore
of resurrection. But my story records
no dormition, no assumption, no paintings
of rose-filled casket amid whitest lilies,
bluest flowers that disciples, startled
and looking skyward, never see.

        And as Tertullian laments,
I live among the living.

Interpreters tell their truths,
their tales, their solipcisms.
None in truth reveals me,
different from any sketch,
spirit hued of dyes no palette mixes,
my life unique, a mystery
beyond theologians' logic,
their controvertible premises.

Entering History

I begin again but not as in the beginning.
Far now from Eden, I enter history,
home first in Sumer, know its cities,
their grids ziggurat-centered, their politics
expansive, warring, failing,
see culture flower for a few decades
on this river-imperiled plain.

To this place I bring my stories,
knowledge of water, its gifts, dangers,
tell of a once-verdant place lying westward,
a *paradise* I say, remembering,

remember too how I made words,
learned to mark them by signs,
to make the useful—basket, wheel,
other tools, and to make beauty
by dyes, strings, hollow reeds, words.
When I tell of reeds, their use,
priests devise stylus, fashion clay
to hand-sized tablets, create cuneiform.

Here I make, work with metal,
lapis, carnelian that brave ships
port to this sea-level place.
In marble I carve my Lady for Uruk,
her high cheeks, incised brow,
gentle countenance evoking presence
I felt in Eden, feel, would honor.

I come to understand my role as instrument
for keeping, change, the woman's part to be,
act, join past to recurring presents.
Entering history I begin this journey.

First-Born Remembered

This miniature is superb in details,
the delicate nails, perfect hands,
skillful thumbs, all wonder
like the new garden.

More than butterfly,
this creation images my soul,
extends it to its new being,
and more than wheel,
this making holds hope,
and I am glad—
        this creation,
        kind of my kind,
        this wonder,
        Cain, child of ample possession.

Redbud

Spring renews with these
coming each April in faith,
brown branches reddening
to bloom, buds radiant
as his blood sourcing
the tree's transformation
from white flowers
to this new color,

tree turned trustee
of his murdered estate
as I hold in trust his memory.

April, all seasons,
he sources my heart
tied in love to him,

tied too in love to my son
his murderer, whose story
lacks the grace of a changeling tree,
who cannot rub his forehead clean
of the mark of his deed, his guaranty.

Grieving Abel, Cain, my sons,
I sorrow at losses, at laws
inexorable and transforming,
this court of the quick and the dead.

After this first human death
I know all others.

Letter to Cain

Though I don't write often,
I think of you, miss you
when fields liven, crops grow,
mature to yield, and in drought season,
river too low to irrigate.
Grain heads poorly now—what's left.
Locusts are our chief harvest.

I'd like to know how your city
planning goes, when the mall opens.
Seth told of triple walls, gates
with panels of our bronze story.

We miss Abel now, always.
The sheep wait him each evening,
cattle search for him in fields
as I do, forgetting.

Your father ages, talks sometimes
of trying for social security.
Perhaps we'll leave this land,
move to Babel.

Seth's home still.
Hasn't found himself, he says,
can't decide what to do.
I work hard, dailiness much with me,
and the familiar palls,
but we make do despite locusts,
remembering Eden, Abel,
how things were.

I'm studying cuneiform,
find stylus handier than reed,
plan to fire our story,
shards of what was, is,

and will, come fall,
garden leavings gathered,
Seth settled.

We love you, long to hear,
want you to take care.   Like a garden,
a city could hold dangers.

Separations

Adam grows weak. I love, tend him
but my touch does not again liven him
resting restless now, breathing labored.

I watch his dying and I grieve,
grieve too for my sons,
for Abel long buried,
for Cain, Seth no longer young
and their fate forecast in Adam,
watch their children flourish
even as they grow toward death.

I know myself *hawwa, the living one*
schooled by Eden, to learn by other pasts,
to live in many presents,
each past, each present, rich
in loss, hurt, wonder, marvel.

Lilith

I knew, know her only by report as my rival,
this night-hag, "first wife," child-stealer.

If Adam found her somewhere
in Eden's reaches or beyond,

she remained his discovery, never mine.
She had no part in his coming forth

nor did she know his life plighted
in marriage, its bonds of troth

with their freedoms,
nor did she know his aging,

sorrow for Abel, new love we found
by mutual loss, our memories of son,

sons, Eden, but she haunts my life
as perhaps she haunted Adam,

by whatever name weds my sons,
offers them a new present of possibility,

her panoramas framing color shots
of the Riviera honeymoon—aging, loss,

the many ways of love yet to discover.
What sons once knew as love of me

survives now in a pale negative,
fading print. My losses here are large

in this erasure of past for inviting rule
of present, anarchic like all *nows*

but full in promise, prospects.
My present too is this. Professional

by long schooling, I try new roles,
practice my lines, study exits, entrances,
how to keep, to let go.

Flood: Noah Remembered

Rain started innocent enough
as children playing in its rarity
and against cautions of mothers
chased near this curiosity,
touched its wide, overhanging sides.

Then sudden rain raged, gulleys rushed
like rivers, currents so swift
children drowned at play, their hands
clutching marbles, balls, effigies.

Resined, sleek, the ark offered no holds,
no space for the drowning who saw
those housed to move on water
float smartly away. Left, the prudent
sought heights, the new islands
made as water claimed land.
The cunning, most able tied planks
together for rafts that rapids
tore apart and splintered.

In the terrible, water-borne menagerie,
greedy Death danced to roiling music,
songs of waters, screams, bays,
trumpetings briefly keening over storm.
Then there was no sound except of water
drowning earth, burying life, all the living.

I see no just cause
for this insensible weather
or for that which felled Eden
except they were.
Find no rationale for the many deaths,
destructions coming even as ark
crowded with the saved,
            I among them,

crossed bitter waters rising
toward a distant mountain
in the postdivulian world,
the many rainbows of that day
the phenomenon of refraction, reflection.

To the Editors of *Who's Who*

Dear Sirs,

Please find enclosed the form you sent
which I can only partially complete.
Few of your blanks save *husband, children*—
    these fill-ins known for ages—
fit my life. I can give no birthdate,
    name(s) of parent(s),
all my education informal, degreeless,
no *honors, dishonors* to quick list,
can check no box of yours as my *profession.*

Elsewhere where I might respond,
space is too limited, e.g., *residences,*
travel, achievements,
which makes me think
your reference book criteria
could allow me at best
a line or two on a thin page
in your next edition.

Had you asked about informal learning,
rare experience, I could write tomes
having seen much—Akhenaton's jerry-built city,
Moses' slow, careful descent tablet-heavy,
Pilate afraid in any storm after sudden
weather change one Friday afternoon.

I've known many rulers of good/bad exempla—
usually the same ruler:
    Sun Kings in Egypt, the Americas, France,
    Charlemagne, the Ottos, Henrys, Georges,
    most of the czars,
    Hatshepsut, Eleanor, Isabella,
    Elizabeth triumphing in her Salamis.

Have known, talked over centuries with the noted—
    Schopenhauer on his fictions of women,
    Greeks sloganing the *comfort of good wives*,
    and *doctors* who shaped, misshaped a faith,
    Wollstonecraft, Mill, others who argued
    to set things right.

Watched in awe as Francis prayed, quieted birds,
    spelled a wolf,
Teresa comforted the sentenced, saw his beheading,
    then cradled his head like her newborn
    as perhaps he was,
heard Merton probe the one we worship,
    dress in varied robes, address in varied rites,

remember too the anonymous to scholarship
whose gifts inform, redeem the daily,
the household truths of our lives whenever lived.

But nowhere, sirs, do these parts
of my experience fit your query,
my inventions never patented,
nothing I wrote, painted, sculpted
copyrighted, all my life free,
open, in the public domain—
    basket, wheel, cave drawings,
    Kamares pottery,
    remedies ascribed to Aesculapius,
    the third temple at Paestum,
    a shepherd's play—these, among others.

You, I expect, would respond that your text
is factual, doesn't seek truth,
is artless, claims no literary merit
though entries must be accurate
within your categories.
This argument is ancient, familiar,
the pedant's quirky, deceiving method.

                  Eve, *Hawwa*

Machiavelli in the Vatican Garden—June 1525

We meet a summer morning, Rome warm
but not seething, arched hedges trim,
populous with birds noising to young—
he an old man, licentious, worldly,
leisured, near to dying, diplomacy done.

He flirts, his talk like the hedges
arch with meanings, his view of woman
clearly Italian. His days now
given to wish, not deed,
and his obsession always with power—
over woman, state, church—
and with powerful he's known,
himself sometimes by coattails
in court of prince and pope.

He knows all about confession
to save a threatened skin, rack of bones.
Of human nature generally, he judges it
a sell-out, best hope to see a few sell out big—
    take-over power play working again.

This he preaches, no flirting now, no grabbing
toward my skirt, his realest lechery always this
lust for, quest of—if never having in ways he wanted—
power in the polis secular or clerical.

Once he dreamed republic, and a Jefferson
given unhistoried land, a continent to plunder,
might have postulated democracy. But he comes
of an old world rich in bad dreams, ancient quarrels,
and chose as best vision, option, gamble,
his thesis of power, prince justified in doing

what princes who survive always know to do—
   a Thutmose, an Augustus, a Julius II,
   a Henry Ford.

Radical thing is he wrote it. Death will keep him
from enjoying his best-seller fame, but his thesis
   sells,
this bedside book of half the world,
this old knight's dream of power
so great he'll forever be kissed awake
by girls lovely enough for the harem
of most durable, richest prince or pope.

Mrs. Milton's Diary

"He married a third wife, Elizabeth Minshull, in 1662,
and spent his last days in what is now Bunhill Row. His
wife survived him."

—Chamber's Biographical Dictionary

Married twelve years, childless (his siring ended
with other endings in the uncivil war),
she's pretty still though little abroad.
Her modest parlor, cluttered but no shrine,
receives few, once-friends dead, fled abroad,
or in new haircuts, collars gone to court.

When I come to tea, we sit beneath favorite
portrait of her late espoused saint,
oval face, wide gray eyes
gazing toward this room he never saw,
nor did he scan her face,
her body except by touch.

Long widowed, she speaks gently of him,
his blind ills, "unmindful" daughters,
last years when body turned infant,
parody of hope lying all before him
where to turn. Slowly, in anger he came
to dependency, having no choice

except his need for her favors.
This she makes clear. "He wasn't
unfeeling for human nature," she says,
remembering perhaps critics, foes,
"but thought little toward people,
more to issues, ideas of God and man."

"And woman, of God as female?" I ask.
"His sentiments are clear," she answers,
"marrying, birthing, tending is woman's all.
He countenanced no heresy as to gender."
"Do you agree?" I ask as she busies
herself with scones, jelly, removing
the mended cozy from the chipped pot.
"Of course, his views were only ideas.
He was like my child, you see. I fed,
bathed, changed, dressed, bedded him,
his ideas of no real effect day-to-day.
As to his beliefs," she adds, "I'm no judge
though his profits, what they were,
were few. I comforted him,
talcumed his flesh that sometimes
pleasured to my fingers. My diary
remarks on these patterns."

I inquire of her diary, "misplaced long ago"
she tells me. I'm sad for its loss.
As she talks, glad for an ear,
I think of golden chain, order broken
at my weak link bringing subservience,
his bad press eager to gender virtue

as male and public, female left the fugitive,
the cloistered. Teatime over, I thank her
for her hospitality, the *Paradise Lost*
he signed with blind fingers.
Thumbing this gift, I find hers,
the small daybook in a woman's hand.

Sons

Their stories are familiar
though happiness we knew in sons
who were almost the first finders
of all first to be found is not elsewhere
remarked, and I would mark it here,
       this joy I recollect

even as I grieve for Abel, for Cain
journeying in a strange land
to found, fashion his harsh, beautiful city
with its lapis inlays, murals of banqueters
tasting victory, their enemies now slaves,
       the nudes in the lowest panel.

I wish to tell in these late days
how it was in the beginning
when they saw, enjoyed, learned
the more than seven wonders
of this world, their world—these babies
who learned to make dark by lifting

their covers over their eyes,
and to make light by taking cover away,
who learned to speak, to name all that
they knew, and to know their names
and their many selves.

Long removed from that time,
I seek to remake it in words,
what it was—the sweetness, charity,
and faith that gave hope
for something of worth
in this making of my own, our kind,
the variorum we are,
that we can and cannot be.

Alias Mrs. Adam

"I have lately come to the conclusion that I am Eve, alias Mrs. Adam. You know there is no account of her death in the Bible, and why am I not Eve?"

—Emily Dickinson,
Letter of 12 January 1846

She serves me Bread Home baked
Finely kneaded as her Lines—
And dressed in bridal White
This snowy Amherst Sabbath
She shows me through Parlor Pane
to her Summer Garden—

Serving its witchcrafted Bees—
Bird halfing Angleworm for Breakfast—
   She did not know I saw—
Hummingbirds spreading from afar
News of Love, its supple Suppings—
And Winter lives here too—
She says—the All transforming Cold—

Confident in her barefoot Rank as Teresa
Angered—passionate as Sappho
Scandaled—she speaks of the Divine, the Lady
Who homes and hides here—revels too—
Reveals Herself in multiple Disguises
None known to Mr. Edwards—

Easy in Sumptuous Destitution—
This Gardener passionate for Life,
Its Creatures, Beings—divines by Sun,
Darkness, Birds, Worms, Flowers—
Their prudent Doings
The Soul of Sun, Darkness—

Bakes Words to yeasty Rising—
Her Spirit, Title, divine,
The Wife—without the Sign—
 Royal except for Crown,
This Eve foregoes her alias
Quick as the Snake old Skin—

Unnamed Mrs. Adam
To claim her christened Name,
This Eve serves us Life—
Death—Lines like a loaded Gun—
Knowing Butterflies' defrauding—
Keen to the Missing All—

She sentences Eternal Dialogue
of Spirit and of Dust—
Called back to her dusty Spirit
And in her Spirit—Faith—
She presents herself demure
While She strokes the All of Time—

The Melody asking "Is *this,
Is Mine* the Way?" to answer "It is!"
And amazed—She knows
We know her Truth.

Schliemann in Eden

He dug there too, of course.
Though I prepared him map,
I warned him his fast trenchings
would unearth little—

what preserves of innocence?
I asked him, but he expected
some remains. Yet most time there,
I didn't know death,

knew no fossils grew in soil
rare for creation. He might,
I told him, find my few inventions—
wheel, knife, chisel—left like spoor

in our hasty flight from flood,
fiery drought I fled
to find new deserts, other soils
to ply for my new deservings.

But no more to find than these.
Nothing save cartography remains
in fact of the garden. Innocence
leaves little trace except in memory.

Though richer than Mycenae,
this place cannot be mined,
I told him, nor pick or spade
unearth, assay its wonder
which was, is, and is other than gold.

Meeting with Dr. Freud

He smokes too much, questions himself
too little, but for me he's endless questions
about origins, my attitudes toward God, Eden,
snakes, Adam, sons, parents—
did I wish to kill my mother?
how do I feel about apples?
　　　Never why did I leave Wien in 1938,
　　　take lodgings in Bloomsbury?

"Please, Herr Doktor," I say,
"believe my origins, unparented as such
and mysterious it's true. I had no mother,
no father as you mean, only this Lady,
this mothering spirit, maker of what was, is,
of my self freed to do, to make in woman's way.
I don't like, dislike snakes, seduce or am seduced
by them. They are, beings and part of creation.
Apples I enjoy, eat, don't think of as *psychosis*.

I repeat—often!—that creation was, is
as I say and I a part of it.
But he disagrees, argues for *complexes*,
diagnoses my *hysteria*, tendency to *autosuggestion*,
wants to *analyze* me, do surgery on my nose
to remedy my *sexual disfunction*.

I reject his diagnoses, his remedies.
He sees my response as *repression, denial*
proving his argument. But I tell him
the true. What I first lived I loved,
but climate without, within made stay
there impossible. I had to do my best
given self, lands, world I had—and did, do.

If, as he says, my dreams betray me, mime
a perfection shut away, I find no betrayal.
All was harmony once—perfection, paradise,
        delight, *delusion* as he names it,
and I'm part and not of its change.

Our conversation goes nowhere, each of us
firm in conviction though our parting is polite,
almost friendly, which is good.
We're to meet at the Woolfs today for tea.

Assisi

"Grant that I may not so much seek to be consoled as to
console, to be understood as to understand, to be loved
as to love."
                                              —St. Francis

Sites made holy by a life are few.
This is one, this open, light place
a locale unlike Delphi or Cumae
where the site implies mystery,

this place alien to desert where Anthony,
cenobites, a pharaoh found truth
hiding in the glimmer of heat, cold.

These Umbrian hills hide nothing,
their pastoral accessible to eye,
their ascent kind to legs, feet,
these hills once home to a saint,
this Assisi, his native town,
which has long traded on his relics,
his legacy that dependencies
of this church keep well-stocked
with goods, friars selling souvenirs.

In the upper basilica, old frescoes wear
loud speakers that cover some, encourage
other cracks. In the lower church,
his grandiose tomb mocks his Lady Poverty,
his bones housed in splendor incongruous
to his life, his faith in more than dogma,
his love that tested, contested theology,
brought modest change and hoped for more.

His love rescued the leper in body, spirit,
and his presence moved the Sultan
whose pagan eyes saw sanctity
in this unwashed vermin-covered man,
his hands, feet, leather-hard and ugly
but God-loved enough for stigmata.
His embrace redeemed nature,
his birds, all living things
freed to unfallen being by his blessing,
Eden's harmony, restored,
its innocence alive in him
who visioned the harmony
that once was.

Leaving the basilica, I pass
booths, vendors with slides,
tiny tiles that parody the frescoes.
I buy nothing, take nothing away
except a glimpse of him
who for a time lived here,
left an aura bus-weary tourists
on a thirty-minute stop sense
as they come from the church
and like the Sultan, find themselves
moved by his presence, love.

Isis Tour to El Amarna

"Thou Ahkenaton art unique. Thy monuments shall
last like heaven, thy monuments like the Sun Disc which
is in it. Thy art unique by the Disc's counsels."

—Hieroglyph from a noble's tomb, El Amarna

Cairo is full of these agencies—
Tut Tours, Osiris Discoveries,
Horus Helicopter Adventures,
Cleopatra's Nights.

I choose Isis, go by Russian jeep
a hundred miles upriver to his dead capital.
While my driver naps dreaming Arabic dreams,
I ferry the Nile where my guide takes over,
pays my Charon.

She's twenty, majoring in Egyptology
at Cairo U. Western dress,
her short-short skirt a new fashion here,
her made-up eyes outdoing those
of tomb-walled ladies, antimony lines
shielding their eyes from sun
as they wait, watch eternity in darkness.

Her specialty, she explains, is Ramses II,
not Akhenaton, but she's "boned up,"
tells me he's "said to be a spirit like world
had never seen before." Warming to her spiel,
she adds, "He astonishes now as then."

She talks about his reforms, the priests
at Luxor, Karnak, Valley of the Kings enraged
by recarved cartouches, old gods dethroned,
their statues defaced by this heretical Pharaoh
preaching his monotheistic cult.

Speaks too of Nefertite, her beauty, power,
disappearance when she's "put away or something,"
comments on his body, his potbelly
that in his reign was model of physique,
ideal for other royals, courtiers, their wives,

comments too on his writings, letters
on wars, disasters, his kingdom's falling apart.
But arrived at El Amarna, she shows me little—
all non-royal tombs long pillaged,
royal tombs near the eastern wadi
destroyed on his successor's accession.

From our perch, she points to desert floor,
finds foundation of one of his many new temples.
I see only sand, his hastily thrown-up city
more hastily wiped out, statues smashed
or recarved with cartouches for the new king,
and old gods people knew reinstalled.

In this twentieth-century sweltering July,
nothing is visible of his singular vision
though this hostile desert evokes his spirit.

> I knew this place long ago, holy
> like Patmos, Assisi, Bonhoeffer's cell,
> and flaming with light of his vision,
> this city the Sun Disc's "Seat of First Occasion."
> The King worshipped, commanded all
>   to worship.
> They did but didn't, attractions of the familiar
>   powerful as always.

> I too would—did—name him heretic. Had he
> made room for Isis spirit in his legend,
> for her making of husband, son, her presence
> as love, life, I would join him in worship.
> But he didn't. Male sun dominant as pharaoh,
> divine by his mother's line.

But I gave—give—him credit for truth
in his partial truth, nearer to true than teachings
of other desert prophets whose eyes saw
a rock-hard god hot for vengeance,
nearer to truth than those who mythed
the divine Lady rich only in lust, caprice.

Always too, the difficulty of translation,
of bringing the holy to the daily.
He was no translator, became, is
a deviation in his Egypt, this present
except as a gloss on a Hebrew text.

Tour done, guide speeds away
rock-and roll blaring her to her village
as I sail back across the Nile, my feet wet,
cool from the make-shift pier,
my legs sand-covered, itchy.
The driver wakes to flies, my coming,
pillages our ice chest for Cokes.
Trip back to Cairo uneventful
except for the ride.

Tomorrow I fly to Luxor, visit the Valley
where finds, mysteries wait,
other pharaohs, queens, sons
to unburial from pillaged,
unpillaged tombs.

Not so here at El Amarna where empty sands
stretch far away, hide no finds,
no shards of an idea almost perfected,
nearly achieved, this notion of the divine
almost achieved by a heretical king.

No other pharaoh left so much,
even Tut centuries safe in rich tomb,
safe now in a museum, gold mask,
gold shoes, gold finger covers all in place.

But El Amarna is nothing now
except testimony to the desert's power,
holds nothing to wrap in wadding,
take away except sand
that the Sun Disc burns
and winds blast toward lush, narrow valley.

Adam at the Supermarket

Once easy in homespuns, he stifles now
in double knit of polyester,
this old man fashioned far from garden

who wanders aisles with his coupons,
searches bargains of world brightly
marketed, platted, tilled, tended

by agribusiness, sea-harvesters,
the seven oily sisters, none Merope loving,
our smoggy constellation obscuring the Pleiades.

Hungry for Thursday specials,
packaged plunder on his shopping list,
he'll carry home basket cases—

store-ripened fruits, grave vegetables,
chicken in fowl parody, plastic fish,
acidic wine, synthetic loaf,

its flavor unleavened—*if the salt
has lost its savor, wherewith*, I say—
but he doesn't hear.

Sweating in chemistried garments,
admiring his shop-window image,
he could ponder his life in split-level,

his swim in chlorine-breathing pool,
senior citizen's pass granting
all access, social security

assuring security of TV, postage-stamp yard
of St. Augustine unnative to Hippo,
phone with caller i.d. to deter nuisances,

hold long and short distances at bay,
easy and not in this reality
of supermarkets selling us faith.

Home, he'll unsack his custom,
flavor purchases for his single lunch,
a spice, herbs for this and for that,

fennel, mint, curry, a pinch of rue,
and always—I pray—a heaping
of rosemary to help evoke what he can't
quite remember or entirely forget.

What the Sibyl of Cumae Told Me
She Told a Painter

"Nights, fussy clerics gone their ways,
I talk freely, glad at knowing how leaves
blowing spell Truth's many presences,
but to you I speak directly, with candor.
You ask, painter, what most amazes
my uttering mind. It is this: Hades
but not as the Mantuan metered the journey.

I'll tell you truly how making my way
to the Gate of Horn, I saw Orpheus descending
in pain, so torn was he by her death, his wounds,
but animals, friends in death as in life,
carefully carried him, his fragments,
the birds guiding, and the stones
    grateful for his marvel in their moving
smoothed themselves to ease this descent.

As I waited, they placed him gently
on ground and they waited
    how long I can't measure
till Eurydice came weeping
and like a mosaic maker
made man out of bone bits, fleshy tesserae.

Then there was dance—
his shady lyre making music
like the spheres moving
as his songs opened this universe to life
and slowly, slowly others came,
remembered feeling, returned as to life
to dance, light feet, bodies drawing energy
from sound, earth, their rhythms
reverberating in all this dark place,

and like an Etruscan priestess, painter,
I danced my way to the Ivory Gate
my tapered shoes moving of themselves,
my body aswirl with motion, becoming, being.

Opening the gate, I saw for the last time
the world I left, saw too the scene I see
in this place. 'Painter,' I said to him
Raphael said was 'lonely as the hangman,'
'Do you know, sir, the source of inspiration
for these blest arising?'"

Tongues, a Tongue from the Past

In this moment, this contemporary,
I think the past, its legacies
distilling meanings to this time,
this America tied millions of ways
to what it little knows, thinks ended.

Listen to tongues of the past, I say,
not just to avoid history's repetitions
but to know more than the local,
eccentricities of this moment,
learn to understand our selves as wrestling
hands bound by subtle, seductive options
many-armed as Buddha's mother
and more enticing, stronger.

Other times had, knew options like
these now, the capricious fate
of a land with unpredictable rivers,
the wars necessary to keep what was,
to expand, be empire like, say, Assyria
or others in nearer times,
immortal conceits of mortal Theban kings,
humane vision, violent practice of Hellas,
stoic maxims defied, deified by Rome.

Such sagas are many, long, and we can
study, translate legacies, opt for the best
from what's called history—*his story,*
her story too—of this world then, now
promising beauty, hope, and their opposites,
this psyche the terrain of the now we inhabit
with our soporifics of leisure,
trust in expanding universe giving all,
our mid-life crises, myth to eschew death,
charity beginning if at all and ending
with us in this now-home as this place is.

As we know the demise of Word,
words sold as babble mute to meaning,
our ears dinning with Babel, deciphering
at best only an occasional voice,

I think of Montaigne puzzling the human,
his society, religion, the massacre,
the riddle of everything—of himself,
of us, cannibals, of nature, its natures.

Sceptic to the end, he kept faith
that these puzzles were worth his while
and that to learn the right question
might be the best answer, required
all his best—all the Gallic gallantry
of his solitary, elegant effort.

Interview at the Plymouth Prep School

Sometimes the lecture circuit repays
its bothers—cancelled flights, same motels,
official meals, valedictory introductions—
with some minutes for saving in memory.

So from these so new to life who image
newness in this old school's protected precincts
    familiar to five generations,
these girls who handle backpacks like pros,
in their cribs wore designer diapers,
but among their questions—
    mostly predictable—what's your age,
    birthplace on your passport, SS#?—
are one or two uncommon.

"Are you alone now?" one asks,
"No," I tell her, them. "First contemporaries
are memories, but I'm kin to all,
to you. When genealogists trace you
to your source, see ancestors shrink in number,
my name will be at the tree's top."

"Why America now?" another asks.
"Why not?" I say. "Possibilities are many
given direction, a better cartography
of what we are. Good maps take work,
care, updating. *Growth* it might be called.
Try thinking your backpacks with Homer,
a history of Western music, a study of Zen,
Chemistry for Humanities Students,
Legacies of Charlemagne are a few
of the world's many gifts finally
to be yours as you know them by heart,
these texts, their hidden texts, question them
by other texts, most by your biography,
the text each of us writes with our life.

This text, your text is your present
to yourself, to those you love,
to the world you live with, in
and leave as heir to your legacy.
For better, for worse, you're intermediaries
in time," I say, "to give to the world as you can."

"How for better?" one prompted
by her teacher asks. "Try humor.
It's not easy but it helps,
can pierce pretense, highlight falsity,
blow away chaff, and laughter
is good for the soul, even prevents
wrinkles in face, in spirit.
Try the cardinal virtues, humility
especially always in short supply.
Believe you in your way can make
a handprint on time, a sign of presence.
Try being Eve, the first woman, the world
your world all before you where to turn."

"Why?" they ask.

"Because you are *Hawwa's* daughters,
and I am."

Perspective

"O, che dolce cosa è questa prospettiva!"

—Uccello

"The misconception which has haunted philosophic lit-
erature through the centuries is the notion of indepen-
dent existence. There is no such existence. Every entity
is only to be understood in terms of the way in which it
is interwoven with the rest of the universe."

—Alfred North Whitehead

Look at it this way: two dimensions
for the dark world, reliefs
brightly painted—banqueting Egyptian ladies
with lotus scenting their waxed wigs;
peasants bringing wheat, cattle,
pheasants; dancing girls fixed forever
in a step the harper's silent music inspires.

Then look at it this way: illusion
from the painter's bag of tricks—
views of Lycabettos, Olympus,
depth of theater space with satyrs
prancing forestage—that opens
the confined rectangles of a villa
at Pompeii landscaped by gardens, pools.

Then look: what they for centuries
taught us to see, the panel containing all—
adoration, battle, portrait bust aware
of the states of soul, Uccello's lancers
aiming to vanishing point, Piero's geometry
finding the third dimension, Leonardo's *sfumato*
hazing over undiscovered lands, souls.

Now see camera view open to our space
showing our planet, all it contains
floating a blue, white, green globe
Galileo couldn't telescope,
    aerial perspective really realized,
this our earth singular as light amid darkness
with mystery its vanishing point.

Then suppose Whitehead's interwoven perspective
is true, that nothing is independent and symmetry
of cause/effect is law more than theory—

then past, present, future bind
almost to Ptolemy's harmonics,
and nothing is singular, alone,
and nothing is ever lost.

It may be then the room opening
to the fresco of Lycabettos opens too
to distant space, to farthest star
astronomers track that lights the villa,
its garden, reflects in the reflecting pool,

livens the New Kingdom pharaoh,
wakens his dark court,
quickens his lithe dancers,
the king, courtiers, servants laughing,
weeping as the harpist plays,

comprises Piero's Madonna,
Uccello's lancers inspired of Euclidean planes,
marvels at *sfumato's* mirages,
perplexes with Leonardo's souls.

The eye trained to perspective
delights in this postulate
sanctioned in probability's gamble,
the mathematician's calculating game,
and confirmed with love,
fear, trembling by us who still
can know Eden and explore
earth, time, self, kin, kind by this view.

Kafka at Santa Elena

He arrives unexpectedly, no introduction,
presents himself awkwardly,
crumpled suit, coughing,
nerves perhaps or weak lungs,

talks excitedly, obviously troubled
by what's happened. Absurd,
he mumbles, telling me how it was,
how it is: why did god do it,

why did you do it, why couldn't you obey
if that was wanted?
Why ruin the garden,
fall to world that's fallen to me—

and on and on, his trial, his trial of me.

No questions now surprise me.
I've had eons to think questions,
ponder answers. None is fool-proof,
any question, any answer—his, mine.

I can't know change the meaning of plan
or my reason for being to make wheel,
learn work, come to pain,
or know change wasn't, isn't.

I accommodate, respond, as we must,
to what is. Regret makes its own reality
though what reality was in fact, in deed
needs reconstruction.

He talks of law, of metamorphosis,
of trying to enter some castle.
I don't deny him these. "K., K.," I soothe,
"your realities I know too,
even your cryptic castle,
and other realities like this *Amerika*, the Big Bend,
are also real."

I can draw him maps
of garden, Cain's city, of Ebla,
Uruk, Akkad, but nothing recovers
the beginning, the many beginnings,
and we must make do as we are.

He doesn't believe, this man
of the modern city, sensitive
to the Jewish question, to questions.
He works he says in insurance.

In the Big Bend—20th cent. CE

"Off the marked trails," he cautioned,
"this park isn't for beginners." Young,
voice soft as cottonwoods ruffling,
he'd mastered the professional smile.
Heading to gatehouse, he turned to add,
"Spanish lore has it that when creation
was done, all extra rocks were dumped here."

I didn't, don't believe his caution,
his translation of another world's lore.
I've followed, follow many trails
marked and not, do here
where creation was, is,
where Joshuas sentinel, yucca fences,
and afternoon shower over,
sotol, ocotillo, wildflowers bloom
in this crevassed land.

Traveling light as always, I camped
at first, then decided to stay, this place
hospitable to its hard life, lives,
to thoughts of past, present. I've come
here by many paths, Assyrian uplands
with no park rangers and many rocks, lions,
by crashing Tyrrhenian seas, their waters
treacherous even for an Odysseus,
by steep ascents, descents in Dolomites,
of Alps, Pyrenees, postcard world
of Switzerland, Bavaria, via the Andes, Rockies,

and by plains as by my first river, rivers,
and the Nile's long journey, wide delta,
and of this new world's old continent,
its spacious tidewaters, Appalachia,

promising plains with sometime crops,
always moving westward like a stout Cortés,
know the path that led Lewis and Clark
to the Pacific, its name ironic and not.

Came by gentle lands, pastorals like Umbria,
Campania, ways, byways of the Loire,
the once-neat streets of Bloomsbury,
its gracious houses now small hotels
with no baths.

After many trails, much travel
reached this Rio Grande, *Río Bravo*,
wild river threading its bend
through an earth-fault canyon
to Santa Elena, this *despoblado* site.

But here too as always,
growing things grow, flower,
animals, people spread across
this vast place are busy
with life, needs, deeds.

Dawns, dusks, I watch summits,
the peregrines, golden eagles
soaring to float on updrafts
dive like birds in a long-ago place
where I first learned nature, my nature.

Night walks show the mountain cat
poised, ears, eyes, nose alert.
Others alert and waiting I don't see
but sense in shadows, brush, as bushes shift.
Days I spot rock-colored snakes
coiled, subtly wound like red whips.

This place speaks truth—
little changes, and here is loss, gain
even as bulldozers noise to ferret
this ancient seabed, harvest its extant dead.

Watching their digging, I see this place
rich in creation, these unearthed bones
once purposed to take on muscle,
stretch scales to wings,
and trusting what they'd never done,
try flight and rise from canyon floor
to sky higher than eagles probe.

Nature directs its will as it will,
must perhaps, as do its beings
though choice enters,
and choice, choices matter.

I home here, journey when I please,
am needed, receive many visitors,
plan to stay, the long-ago garden I seek
in time, story, change, in self, selves—
          wholeness never complete—
always to seek, try to make,
perhaps to be again in this place
where I am, have my kiva,
this Santa Elena where I, Eve
now, always, again begin again.

Honor
Card
and
Other
Poems

Part 1

Photographing the Facade

San Miguel de Allende

They are eternal as angels and demons.
Wrapped in clothes gladly rags,
holding out for coins their antique hats,
they wait as they always wait,
these same beggars everywhere

at every church we visit:
the gaunt Indian mother nursing
a gaunt baby, the archetype
of lameness, and one whose flaying flesh
is rebus of pain.

A few miles away the freeway runs,
motels transmogrify the landscape,
and even on this square, plastics
and polyesters conquer market
where American Express buys us everything.

Yet these who waited surely
for Cortés before monuments
to other gods are constants,
and we who would take the facade
aim Polaroid higher, tilt viewfinder

to seek Saint Michael putting down
the pink, wounded stony demon
and triumphing as he always must,
frame from film these wounded
lingeringly as Satan, as Christ

in some eternal and relentless scheme
that none of us does fully cause,
cannot resolve, and embarrassed
by irresolution, we search
with narrow focused eye
for Gothic things.

The Lie and Truth of This Land

It's been tricky getting here: starting
basically with no directions, we circled
left and right through cul-de-sacs
in icy and fierce geographies.

Bonded, trothed, we foraged separately,
each army wanting provender
        and uncomfortable
in bivouac. Von Clausewitz too we left uncut,
fooled of fickle, rare Corinthian weather,

and when our armies met, war was guerrilla.
You were good at hiding even in bare land,
but I'd skills for ferreting your defenses,
seeking keenly in private terrains.

Your tactics ran too often to waiting,
and I was primed always to quick muster,
knives bone sharp, thrusts apt to cold jungles
though some victories tasted like defeats,

the cooking sad after butchering,
and our incisions festering, we helped,
had to, each other drain wounds.
When we circled with meager compass

fretting northward, children sniffled
edgy of battleground, parents cheered
our skirmishes, friends—they laughed.
After campaigns, usually on weekends,

there were Mondays to be got through:
work, school, grocery, money-changers
intruding preemptorily enough:
if compass couldn't guide, necessities did:

do: it would be nice to think the battles over,
jungle clothes for arctic guerrillas
packed with permafrost away, cul-de-sacs
mapped straight as interstates. They're not:

any moment compass can explode, spin
expiry to our brief order, terrain invite
guerrillas to maiming though less now
we respond to these invitations.

If we've staked no south fields
bountied by gentle flowers, more now
other, unnorthern needs avail:
we're less proud, having been

often wounded, much defeated,
and I at least am afraid of the cold.
I'm weary of wrong compass, battle weather.
If not love, it's more love than hate,

and most days I'm amazed at our arrival,
come by circles, foolish turns,
icy, dulling combat to this tricky place,
the lie and truth of this land,

Corinth lush beneath deceiving tundra,
our armies mainly easy at armistice
and rarely foraging, commissaried now
mostly from home.

Two on Gulliver

Mrs. Gulliver at Home in Newark

She managed well her years of waiting,
this Mary Burton, second daughter
to Edmond, hosier in Newgate Street.

Though homing carried comforts,
it had work, mysteries enough as she coped
with debtors, moves, children,

his absence, no letters coming
from worlds beyond posting—and with him
home, these returns hardest, the voyages,

their effects alien to her native ways.
His first trip back, he fondled her
like a kitten, a doll, kept wanting her

to walk on his hand, find the sheep tucked,
he said, in his pocket. After second trip,
he shouted each day her grossness,

then crept to her breast like a babe,
frightened by night, the sound of wrens,
terrified of the circus monkey.

After the third voyage, was he mad
she wondered, talking of sunning cucumbers,
of living forever yet yearning death,

demanding her beside him every night
to leave her in late pregnancy
and fly to captain the mutinous ship.

When he came back smelling of horses,
in amity only with stallions,
she kept to duties, tended her children,

fearful of whinnying father. At first
she'd have dressed like a groom
to talk with him, to comfort this yahoo,

but he'd no speech for her, and she thought,
came to think, her world worth probing,
navigation treacherous, navigator a novice.

After making meals, lessoning children,
she turned bookish, kept a journal, wrote at
            poems,
came hardly to note his whining, snuffy
            swoonings,

and finally grew eager for his returning
home to horses. She discovered a new country,
its solitude, her self requiring little dialogue,
no voyaging to fit his far-fetched worlds,

and even when Stella called with talk
of the curious Dean, the best moments came
after, the hours left to her jottings,
to quiet, her feathery bed singly quilted.

Gulliver Stabled

Finally his reason knew no limit,
learning from Emmanuel aborted,
common sense deserting him

apprenticed now to horses.
Thus returned to Newark,
he berthed in stable, forsaking

ancients and moderns to write the tale
no one believed, not even Mary,
his fearful children. Speaking only

with stallions, his speech at last
the nasals of Houyhnhnms,
he held to his flaying vision

knowing such flaying him altered him,
all appearance for the worst.
Fierce indignation tearing his heart,

he held to ironies too, the envelope
with the lock of her hair,
the locket engraved *cogito ergo sum*
enfolding miniatures of his children.

Credulous, a gull fishing geographies
uncharted by any map, he did as he could,
his manifest invoicing the terrible epiphany
of all perverse in his upright heart.

Sometimes late in night, measuring
with the two sight vanes of pelorus,
he thought on misanthropy,
pondered topographies of pride,

wondered on Mary, Captain de Mendez,
toyed with cartographies kinder
than reason and explored, compass
fixed to love's cold star.

But nothing came of this.

Mornings brought word on England,
Ireland, all their slops,
news of Vanessa dead, Stella ill,
the Dean melancholy, traveling
to madness, eyes, ears, mind contorted.

Stabled, Gulliver held to his yieldless vision,
this sanguine man to whom misanthropy
wasn't indigenous and who in reason
should know hate only as a singular fruit
of a swift, deciduous season.

home economics: a marriage poem

we signed up with high hopes
that mayday. no signals sang
distress though early June
showed our economics unmelding.

you believed categorically
in the invisible hand sweeping,
washing cups, smoothly oiling
what smiled in our marketplace,

and i leaned Keynesian,
deficitly spending disaffection,
stocking heavily in fool's gold
yet yearned to buy the realty of home.

you named this too your intent
though your methods required wealths
only nations provide, and my principal
was mortgaged at too low interest.

such economies computed this Argonne,
siege city in these Trojan walls,
our Gettysburg where daily you outflank
me. i'm inflated, you depressed

with our gross markets, high war profits.
my visible hand would scorn its pyrite,
and you want, convince me you do,
smithing better than your forgery

of Adam. these home economics
need all domestic science to allay.
yet mayday has, can have, other meanings
than distress, my friend, and i distressed

call you, your help, our help, call
my friend, my little friend.

to philomena uncanonized

"Philomena's official demotion finally came as part of a
long-term program . . . to tidy up the liturgical calendar."

Time

we who named you saint
unsaint you; born of our history
we unhistory you, never sturdy
like Teresa noising
on Avila's discalced stones,

or Catherine evangeling stridently
in Siena and exiled Avignon,
you had no tongue
nor even tapestry
to tell your story.

bones were your only plot
though you sourced, quietly it's true,
miracles enough: healings,
visions from which nuns wove
your uncloistered fame.

now expunged, lacking myth,
you grave in secular casket
unfriended by clerics,
cautious laymen though still
perhaps saint and friend to God

constant above his images
and embarrassed at the hasty
rechristening of your old statues,
fast dyeings of your glassy myth
even as he knows now, always

your true legend, holy ghost
whose worth adds its glow
to wax quietly as candle
timeless and unflickering
within his enduring light.

Street Child: Ciudad Acuña

I have been seeing him
as he has me
all our years:
boy slight, eager-eyed,
dirty hands holding Chiclets
that will metamorphose to shoeshine kit
and then to trays with jewels
of paste and metal
too greenly fraud for belief;

and I, gringa bringing money,
come this weekend to barter
crafty bargains in this border town,
drop silver in soiled hands
and see quaintness vanish as need,
greed coil fingers like snakes
and spirit gluts itself
on a sacrament of coins.

This our brief encounters occurs
as we are cornered by frenzy
of horns, cars deadly as bullets
racing the weekend streets,
and momently together in peril
we wait, I the American glutton for goods
and he the street child selling—
or so roled we seem.

The view is existential, and home
tomorrow putting away my gains,
I will think of none of this,
no vision to intrude of exchanges
better than our tradings, of words,
acts that might have offered more
than our easy, cheap mutual defrauding.

French and France

for Charlotte Benard Combs, tutor

You won, you know,
and you'd be pleased.

Those long afternoons of supposed French,
you were of course schooling them,
your fortunate heirs,
my daughters,
but in something more than only language—

rather in a lover's demesne,
an inherited estate as lasting
as mystery of sources
and as absent from being
as you since your heart's revolt,

and this summer,
their first journey in your land
they travel mostly your mappings:
Charlemagne yet kings generously,
always mindful of honor, Roland;
and William, conqueror, never bastard,
commands your bony kin
to craft his sturdy towers.
In Burgundy, yield of ancestral vines
stills to dark wines delectable
beyond nectar, and chocolates
(casual of cavities,
you filled girls with these)
softer than butter, better
than highest cuisine
wait in shops
rich as your foretelling.

What I see, show them, they see
and polite, these daughters,
do not dispute. But vivid
beyond vista of our transient summer
is your sweet France,
in transformation so splendid
it could exist (and did)
only in memory,
yours selective as kindest lover's.

You'd be surprised how well
you taught and how faithfully
they learned your lessons—
not just verbs, vocabulary
but your real subject, your France,
to which you guided them by maps
better than Michelin's.

As I watch them, my daughters,
I envy you those late afternoons
when you won them,
won for them
this winsome country
grammared in beauty,
syntaxed by claim of love
sacred and legended as Roland's.

Vacationers at Amecameca

A clear focus we wanted,
so guidebook guided
we left the flowery market
to climb the sudden hill
remarking the rocky stations
of the Indian as Christ,

remarking too the pilgriming,
the old signing their Sunday black,
the young in white or gaudy
as violent rainbows.

From the top, we said,
we would see volcanos unclouded,
envisioned how their snows
would reign in the high sky

but saw in fact only this site

shrine housing him who
we guessed
once walked this hill
with message they accepted
and heard preached again
by his crystal-tombed cadaver
brown as dried leaves
rustling in their demise.

The hill we'd read
is famous for its view.
We came for this
but at crest found only relic
whose lore we couldn't hear
and saw only seeming snow
of volcanos we knew easterly
but could not for clouds see.

Helen Unlored

One moment there
must have been
brief by its brightness
before desire despair
knowing terrible beauty
before they who saw
and she who was
learned and reckoned
as they must
her fatherhood of God
and brotherhood to man

before the drama was
from which legend came
that uncomprehending
we can neither ignore
nor forget.

One time at least
there must have been
before the lore began
when perhaps even she
was graced in innocence
favored by only loveliness

far away the day
when old men at Troy's walls
remarked in wisdom
on her beauty
and counted beauty's fates

a time when no reckoning
seemed needed
and beauty was attended
by nothing else at all.

Traveling the Outback

He's only modestly a dog,
hardly bigger than a cat
and comfortable in petness.
Yet dreaming he turns canine:
lying sideways on my bed,
he imagines wildness.

Inch ants, beetles, galah
cockatoos demand his discipline.
Emus need chase.
His sleeping feet move miles
over the Outback's hot sand.

Dingos scare, bay in longing
toward desert moon,
and as wild camels rush our camp,
he shelters under bush
stickered as blackberries
to guard his hard-won game.

Hunting desert rats, he's better luck,
his reality of mouse
triumphantly transformed,
growl from his hungry throat
heralding sweetest victory.

As springs creak,
he yearns for springs,
the curious wells,
even sight of Indian Ocean.

Thirsty now, he whines himself awake,
passported by need back to our world
where outback is back yard,
and the only dingos near
pad in the zoo eternity of cages.

As caged to me, he comes awake,
all wildness left its wilds,
and pet, he licks my hand
as I give him his comforts,
water bowl, favorite jerky,
cakes of bony fiction, his dream
pristinely lost to this reality,
freedom's wiles, most fears bartered
for comforts of his, my familiar prison.

waking to the late news

turning from dreamy reality,
i hear the midnight song-and-dance
of some 40s movie; see Betty Grable,
Dan Dailey frolic in black and white,
the living color fled.

then across their tapping, whitest
shoes, frames of their still lives,
teletype brings words:
sleep riddled, glasses buried in covers,
my eyes lose, grasp letters
as the words tap away
until boldest fonts proclaim
MILLIONS MAY DIE—
STAY TUNED FOR MORE NEWS!

i cannot stay tuned, my strings
unstrung, eyes spangled
with this elegaic dancing pair,
our mutual 40s lost, its life
resurrected only in history's colors.

tuneless, my years danced away,
i probe this celluloid shard—
did i really dress like that?
wear a cheerleader's sweater?
did i bounce when I walked?—
but i don't stay tuned for answer,

for these millions who may, will
i know, die. only the immediate
catastrophe is missing—the legend
i believe, long awake from any dream
of an RKO happy ending as waking,

turning to dream, i always sense
this presence tapping over Betty and Dan,
over all us millions, tapping gravely
through our slippery hours
its dance of our late news.

omnibus

the glimpse is only a minute:
driving past the bus,
i see her,

pink scarf tied under chin,
white hair an unruly halo,
her pose instinct with age.

she could be Rembrandt's mother,
but she isn't: is mine and alone
though the bus ferries many.

'i must reach her,' i say,
'ride with her to her stop,'
but no message gets through to her

or to my foot unwilling to brake.
sight commutes to pictures
moving as i watch the conductor

come to her, his guard-dog
silently barking
(the panes give him three heads)

though she never sees the dog,
hardly notes the conductor
seizing her fare, punching

her ticket for this journey.
movie still running, i plunge on
at my own speed knowing in fact

i will catch her bus another stop.
meanwhile, traffic encircles
and the only way to go

is with its irrevocable motion
as she goes on alone as she must
to where the bus is taking her.

Part 2

Museum Scene: An *Adoration*

Look you there, magus,
you farthest from the child
and kneeling, knees creaking
slightly it's true.

See, sir, toward the child
looking as to speak,
his face centered in light
and his countenance smiling
at you awkward in your posture.

Let the posturing go, sir,
and look to his comfort.
He would you would see,
word his ease at this stable,
beasts breathing warm on him
and arms of his mother crossed
gently to brace his limber back.

His eyes show well enough
he knows
as she doesn't yet
that afternoon
even to thirst and the spear.
But now
in the perspective of kind time,
chiaroscuro working its truths,
joy too is his province,

and courtesy requires, sir,
that you bone-tired
of your dubious journey
look to more than knees,
see beyond pigments of paving
to him centered in light
that reaches out to touch you.

Antediluvian

Meteorology wasn't then perfected
nor was the weather
though aching bones foretold
and eyes scanning skies finally
must have found clouds.

Not, though, when he started,
this novice of arks
hammering all the skyblue days
and worrying clear, cold desert nights
with his busy mitering.

Disoriented in dry violent world
by vision of violent waters,
he crafted gopher wood
to shape sufficient for safekeeping
and gathered to sanctuary enough
of earth and sky for paradigm.

Absurd as any Dane
he leapt to faith in floods
on soil watered only by mirages.
As camels sweating, fly-troubled
moved annoyed at his noisy carpentry
and neighbors mocked him, architect
of vessel anchored on dry land,
his pure heart willed one thing
to which this amazing ark was witness.

Frivolous he must have seemed,
building a desert boat useless
as boats in bottles, and eccentric,
so unlike other men
it's said he walked with God
angered by concentric multitudes,
and heroic, bargaining to save
what God despaired of keeping,

jand human, the drunkenness
born of his visionary deeds
flooding his dry, salvaged world
to command, torment
his last god-haunted days.

Triptych

In the Flemish Room

Postcards don't shrink them much,
these miniatures of pain;
the oily flesh real enough for strigels

on these busy canvases telling whole
legends of their saints:
wheels spin, arrows pierce,

and the flaying, oh that's the shock,
knife separating flesh from skin
the executioner tears away,

pulls off to leave the red thing
the right panel shows. Eyes, though,
of this martyr, all Flemish martyrs

are all the same
even when cross is means:
the startled look of saints,

'hast thou forsaken'
seeking to speak in pigments
centuries old:

the startle at pain certainly
(this reality usually surprises),
the startle too that now is time

of dying, perhaps to glory
the eyes say, ask, yes, to be martyr
that is the question, the mystery
their death will or won't answer.

Uccello's St. George: Interpretation

He saw in proper perspective:
his St. George poised for dragon,
its fire at vanishing point
of its fierce impotence, and the lady
serene though leashed to dragon
transfixed for agony.

Allegory by color too is proper:
George's green saying laurels
for the church, the dun, enormous beast
the pagan hordes, the white gowned lady
telling natural goodness
the sacraments can by grace redeem.

Possibly too there are other meanings:
Uccello, friend of the Medicis,
must have interpreted widely,
and possibly,
just possibly
the lady leashed to dragon
is indeed a lady leashed to dragon:

serenity may be her mien
but manners change
and white stains easily:
her dragons are real
and the leash is as strong
as the sword and more binding:

and even if one unwieldy dragon
is gored, others hide over mountains
in smoky background curling fretfully
and no George can slay them all:

I can believe this lady, my lady,
leashed to dragons,
and I can believe too
leashes are stronger than knights,
than swords or sacraments of mail.

goya, his matador

it's the eyes you see
he saw

　　　　that see the decades
　　　　of bullfighting done

　　　　leaving him witness
　　　　to truth of thousands
　　　　of bloodlettings,
　　　　the beasts, his own,

　　　　no mysteries left him now
　　　　except eternal ones.

　　　　horns of the deadly
　　　　and death wounded
　　　　wounded him well enough
　　　　that he survived in a way

　　　　and his eyes
　　　　somber, wise, telling,
　　　　speak from dark palette
　　　　the true color of things.

Cézanne and Mont Sainte-Victoire

"the stirring climax of Cézanne's art"
Cézanne: The Late Works

Yes, he did move a mountain,
this mountain as stroke by stroke,
he raised its granite toward canvas.
Years and years he worked

harder than housemovers,
his task bigger,
and his moving moved slowly,
so much to unlearn, learn.

Early, foregrounds dominate:
axial almond trees, houses,
roads decompose; palette dead-ends.
Then toward the end he was seeing

how to do it, paints become
pulley, brush steady for lever,
Egyptian mechanics working
even for mountain sized beyond pyramid

and so indivisibly itself,
its integer demanded all
his wholeness. To move such mass,
he slowly learned

the angles to brush, the stable ground,
primary geography of Mary's color
and when finally toward the end
his vision moved the mountain,

he discovered the simplicity
of its innocent form whole, unquarried
enduring in his holy victory,
its victory in his wholly enduring.

Gloss

Falling asleep over
"Falling Asleep over the Aeneid"
I dream you resting aside me
suddenly companioned
in my bed.

I look you, patrician head,
lonely profile, eyes troubled,
and your convenient instrument
(we are prelapsarian as Eden)
unchallenged by my likes.

We talk you and I
of loves, ancestors, God,
madness come of knowing
too much who exactly one is
and not liking the one.

A common plague we decide:
if heritage carries this disease,
so too does my new country,
plainly frontier
but contagious with it.

Histories long and short
all have abysms—
we agree in our easy talk—
mad sanity finds us in any locus
even beds feathery as gardens.

I dream you comfortably,
turning you like pages
skin smooth as bond,
body careless as loose quartos,
mind scrutable as boldest Garamond,

and am shocked to hear you say
"we've never met" (you're right:
except for the meeting of poems),
and swift as Aeneas urgent to move
beyond shamming gates of ivory

you escape my dream
and I wake
to think you like all my loves,
fancy more than real, easy
only in my fanciful conspiracy.

Unsleeping now
I turn abed to touch
your version of the honest truth,
these anxious runes
of your harsh, chilly poems.

For Xanthippe: Praise

To you, Xanthippe, I offer praise,
recompense for ills centuries laid
upon your bourgeois aims, ridiculed
by Xenophon, gossiped in Alexandria
keen to scandal you Platonic goodwife.

If in fact Socrates proclaimed
having married you he could then stand
anything, he spoke as Greek
poor in chivalry but rich in wit
to phrase the partial wiseness
that is philosopher's truth.

Tending children, knowing what food
ample for meal, its when and where,
making places for sleep, carding
for cloth to clothe your family—
these tasks, none lofty, are requisites
for welfare general and private

allowing some few the leisured
evenings of philosophy,
its long symposia a quest
for fine if abstract goodness, holiness.

Never espousing its goodness, holiness,
housewifely code can never canonize
though I've known a few fair women,
all unremarked, martyred by this creed
as fatally as by any gridironed
or hemlocked dying, and something

needs remarking of you, keeper
of what mundane order obtained
in your house, for enduring and not
his daily, nightly needs, for carrying

to birth the sons you raised,
and for lasting even with marriage to martyr.

I like to believe that shrew if you were,
you had provocation and knew
that husbanded by Socrates,
you had stood almost everything.

Though it's late and past recovery
of your good name, I offer to you,
your homely virtues these homely words,
my bourgeois, mundane praise.

Dr. Johnson's Crocodiles

He is one of my sources
and I think him often:
most by Boswell's lexicography
and sometimes by sources his own.

Words were his true source,
and language ways he knew firmly
though it's said knew
"not so much where the word came from
as what norms ought still
to be guiding":
thus his crocodile
swampy in etymology
as "the saffron-fearing beast."

Seeing crocodiles today
lazing at the zoo—
they are always lazing—
and dumb to become
their wordly fate,
I breathe to sluggish ears
their wondrous surprise
out of Dr. Johnson

and magically, suddenly swift,
syllable-shattered from sloth,
their wide teeth useless
and chattering like rabbits,
in tears now only for themselves,

they flee in flight before me
come in this lexical hour
to tell their fortune in saffron,
the changeling vegetable gold,

as they discover themselves
transformed to sentience
by spell of word: these
once slumbering solid
and impervious as rocks

transformed by news of crocus
to search on wide savannas
their mystery of being
fleshed by word.

# of some recent dead

1.

how do you Mister Death
like e e
cummings at you

coming with lyrics and loves
into your really enormous room
coming wide-eyed and word handsome
leaving legatees busied
computing his one-time equations
deciding on the tulips
of his puddle-wonderful
and periodless world

how do you like your blue-eyed boy
who has even now
enough higher octane
of estlin and edwardian essence
to transform oysters to pearls
sweeping into your narrow realm
        best suited to Cambridge ladies
ready to convert its missing all
into whatever Serene Illustrious
        and Beatific
if to be found by this Lord of Creation
Poet

2.

Where walls fall and nothing gold can say
your dying reminds us of all going
as ash not gold on a path to a yellow wood
after spring pools, snow fields, diverging roads,
colts, tramps, masks, your old man's icy night
dark by your ironic displacing,
you who so well described this world
you'd expect only unease too in any other.

And going now our miles toward sleep,
we uneasy with pastures and runaways,
woods and desert places, learn the landscape
of your world as rich in fright as love,
pain as beauty, mark your wise, wry, frosty
cautions that say there is in fact no stay.

3.

Who traded in words wheelbarrows
daisies medicines is now beyond such barter.
Trips to contagious hospitals
booted no end of contagion
except for brief isolated cases
and no physician we know
can finally save or ever could

yet within inevitables
spanned spanking to life
comforting to death,
you patterned of Rutherford,
Paterson ways older than oldest Jersey
citing many wholenesses
and many ails and woundings.

Now scribing and prescribing done
you leave what caduceus cannot wand away,
earthy lines mythy as Hermes, roots
branching in spring to spring to new life.

4.

to join these now
you come politic cautious meticulous
full of high sentences somewhat obtuse

decorously dying
in the London winter
to appropriate burial east of Coker

having come a long way
by whatever measure
from St. Louis
to greet the Eternal Footman
and learn at last
about give sympathize control

as in our rooms
critics, biographers come and go
talking of Mr. Eliot so
bidding quick, troubled good nights
to your long, troubling life, poems,
hurriedly summing you up
because for us, please
it's still time.

5.

how do you Mister Death
like these poets coming
still limbed once life bright
world and wordly wise
who guised, smithed sturdy realms
of their/your/our doings
these makers crafty
even about this enormous you
and your enormous night and/or day.

Republic Revisited

He was right to distrust it:
poetry is a lie
not to be brought to truth
by makers' confessions
or exposed beyond narrowest limits
by scholar-critics, the philosopher's craft.

Like his cave, forms, his postulates,
it sustains itself by its web
of words woven to metaphor
and lured to reel by limning.

He was right, of course,
to distrust it and to spin
as argument contrivances
so obvious only philosophers
could believe them:
no poet or maker of beds
finds this sophistry
convincing.

Unlike poets, Plato I believe
believed his metaphor
with only the philosopher's part
of his brain. He knew, we know
the brain has many others.
Poets have as their chief defense
how totally they are liars.

poetry and post, texas

out of a high school writing contest
what miracle is wrought
except a poet whose land
is jackrabbits big as coyotes,
mesquites with china roots,
and dust bowling over dust
though sun lanterns
and stars lacquer the wide sky.

he's never seen a daffodil
nor does Pecos flow like Avon,
yet this marvelous boy manned of language
visions his landscape whole.

jackrabbits graced as unicorns
roam these lines
where mesquites laurel their prickly legend,
and dust, sun, stars metaphor his universe
full of bad typing, worse spelling,
and overcome by poetry.

sick of paltered lines
on paltry passions, i find
these lifting craft to heaven's gate
and ringing by his sight.

it's not enough to judge he's won:
he's by God a poet, and Post
and all West Texas
can never be proclaimed again
the same.

Part 3

Program Note

"I live in almost continual vexation, envy, and
persecution."

J. S. Bach

I posture in my listening attitude,
cup hand to face, ignore program's loss,
watch him maneuver fingers, stops,
feet to sound this

the Kapellmeister wrote amid fathering,
householding, churching as in Leipzig,
teaching choir boys Latin, flattering nobles,
counts, kings, tempering well the Klavier,
fashioning Anna Magdalena her book,
remembering some harpsichord to do
for the Saxony elector, and making—
finger bruised, sensitive to pen, keyboard—
our music amid vexation, envy, persecution.

Amid vexings, envies, persecutions,
persecutings, I listen unlisteningly,
watch the organist move his head
to measure as sunbeams play fugues
on his back and metallic blinds
kaleidoscope shapes on hall walls,

but make no music or words
or love or life, have only
this half-life of posturing,
as here of listening, always doing
and always of doing nothing.

Observing myself restive,
I look in earnest to the keys,
wonder where to sup and if to sleep,
and note relieved this program
better tempered than my flat being
almost to the 30th variation.

For Frank, Lost in the China Sea

"How small a part of time they share
That are so wondrous sweet and fair."

Edmund Waller

Like that Greek day
so I imagine
was his,
a day of provisioning brightness
marked on earth
by full summering raiment
and in sky
by calm winds
all rudeness suspending
and beneath, smoothest sea.

Like Icarus
he too felt triumph
so machined, wax-welded
moving feather light
till fell battle trickery
wounded the metal,
and wanton, curving,
plane revolted from pilot
to spiral, a silver sliver falling.

Instrument panel rioted
to proclaim this fall,
numbers confirming
the brittle sea waiting
braking
this fragile craft,
its brittle bone parcel

as sky-dropped craft
broke calm water
and gulls fish-scanning
noised a benediction.

Now in this Texas season
gaudy with Judas,
orchards in flame,
pears in communion dress,
I hear of that plunging moment
and would remark his Icarian
unlegended descent
sharpening in blunt words
feelings not of kin-grief
but keen at loss of him
once student, then pilot and dead,

wonder if he who read
of warring heroes struggling
sirened seas was schooled
in whatever ways of poems
for his heroic fall;
if play of monarch battle
instructed him for games of war
played out in blood and dyings;

hope the lyrics,
sweet sad jeweled songs
of the fair young gone,
which he read most young and fair,
seemed prescient,
made time more dear,
spoke truth he heard
in their true, uncomforting words,
and that in time of falling
panic was not all his crew.

Girls in the Rain

Carrying shelter, they move carapaced
like swift turtles gaily shelled,
not huddled, these school girls,
but walking boldly their slippery steps
and nourished it seems by rain they flee.

From office view,
I've noted for years their migratings,
confusing warblers alighting
each fall in this place,
watch these of this season,
their umbrellas a shell game
all win and lose.

Quick here they come and go,
feeding in this field, these classes
to find our knowledge wanton,
teaching by their presence
exempla of beauty to us
professing its abstracts.

In our words and nominal tone
they find such madness
as dooms Cassandras to frenzy
that these, so many Helens sheltered
in youth enduring as their beauty,
may in courtesy hear
but whose grave argument
they need not now at least
believe.

Trees and Progress

This is their last spring, these trees,
and untutored by hollow-eyed houses
with jacks as new foundations,
these soon to lie earth level
bud, their branches gold
in promise this warm afternoon.

Borers, ants might have worded them
their doom. Progress too sends messages
but not such as trees can hear, heed,
and this afternoon, they stand
apriled and foolish, budding, leafing,
brilliant in their confidence of June.

housebuilding

people who build glass houses
ought to have thought of the birds:
when walls of glass sit
so that from angles fliers come
nothing opaque suggests barriers,
birds in flight crash on these hard panes.

seeing familiars, trees, sky beyond,
these innocents about nature and vacuums
reckon as empty this glassy space
that is our house
and fly into the crystal sheet
to bed on deck or ground,
bones so askew and feathers scattered
we sometimes don't know
who they are.

this has happened many times
and supports speculations about sight
            and sense,
nature's ways and ours,
but always i'm sorry for these birds
unwary of our tricks with sand
and wish we could post and they read
a sign that says Birds Beware or Glass, Alas!

housebuilding taught us much
about foundations, need for sealing
to slow the falling apart,

of water's certain downward flow
even through ground-level room,
but their crashing, dying
is the most expensive knowledge—
   emotionally i mean—
housebuilding gave.

as with much else of wounding
and measured in pain, losses,
i'd change our house
were it to do over
to a darker, warmer place,
more hospitable to insight
and less inviting to hurt
by its hard and optic illusions.

uses of nature

uses of nature are adverse and not
i'm reminded by season and history.

winter barely festivaled
before quince, forsythia flower
garishly celebrate
this Lenten weather
as amid rocks weeds spin,
bulbs green the ground,
sticks bud, birthed
in adversity and not,
aided sometimes by our nurture.

history too tells stories of nature,
of us and nature.
because they are omnipresent,
i think of sparrows and a story
of sparrows and war,
of some general in China
who doused sparrows with kerosene,
set them aflame, and loosed them
over villages he would take and did.

the burning birds mad to flap out
flames flew, fell groundward,
their brightness falling on roofs, yards,
homes, barns, animals, people,
all changed as by Medea's magic
to a sorcery of inflaming.

uses of nature intrinsically
are of birth and dying
and nature is always adverse and not,
and we upset by too much use either way.

i think of the burning sparrows
as parable of our wanton ways
east and west, feel remembering
this old story in this May
lush enough for most greedy,
gluttonous sparrow guilts
of my own, akin to my kind.

geese at dawn

they storm this November sky
in torrents of cloudy wings,
throats shrill as mad prophets.

lost to disorder, these hundreds
of birds seek to find how to go,
a direction to end their circling,

random motions, accidents,
skirmishes in this characterless dawn.
flying again and again over places

they rested last night, they keen
their need for right sight,
for eyes looking ahead guided

by feathers leading the flock
in its isosceles of flight.
but current blinded, betrayed

by these cold skies, they turn,
pivot in this dizzy air echoing
their chaos in this unsettled day.

reduced circumstances

the barbering's skillful—
that can be said for it:
a lock gone there, a follicle here
sealed in its vault and dead
to re-being; and the color,
brown gone white so goldenly
i hardly saw it,
eyes neither what they were.

all things considered
it's been a dexterous manicuring,
nails hardening at rates
beyond clear filing away,
and muscle tone washed to fat
on shores of fatigue
so plush and sleepy
i never noticed.

but i do:
quick sight reflected
in department store window:
and am too suddened by loss
for any buying.

what happened
and when
that this is me

debauched, reduced
to this state that optimist
i always slouchy in spine
could never on darkest day
imagine
and this day is bright.

cuptowels

hanging in the sun
their past comes through
the feed-sack dyes
of Plymouth rocks
cackling history
fabled as their being.

shrunk of their seeds
and raveled of their curious seams,
sacks washed and sunned
waited mothless cedared months
for translation to treasure:
print sacks to shirtwaists of copious hems
and to bonnets for babies
who might melt in the sun;
scraps of every shape
put away to patchwork quilt
for millennial everydays.

but the domestics still told
their tales through lye
that never quite worked
however strong,
and their destiny
plebian and inevitable
as drudgery neolithic to our day
was cuptowels.

these hang now amid my wash
remnantly telling how
one sycamored afternoon
swinging in leisure on her porch
she bordered this sack cloth
with cross-stitch, appliqued
busy Dutch girls on, and almost
transfigured this native cloth

to fable of Netherlandish being
except for dyes of triumphant hens
never quite purged by bleaching:

now on my clotheslines bedecked
with polyesters synthetic as detergents,
these hens beyond all lyeing
parade, mighty shades bloodless
and real, these stitched and fabulous beings
evoking in their durable lines
the marvel of life alive in tumular stories.

pronoun

lacking reference
and wanting antecedent,
i seek nouns,
nomenclature, referent
by which i gain
meaning, definition;

look imperatively
within sentences
declarative,
interrogatory, and more,
backward too in old laws
of grammars and forward
to some transforming scheme

as i stand grammarless
caught in relentless present
progressing in tenses,
undone by punctuation,
and in uninflected language
seek modifiers, but meanings
are misplaced somewhere,
leaving words to dangle
like threads too fragile
for grammar, sentences
too frail to hold any meaning.

Scene

Don't scream the dragonfly away
> stopping a moment busy wings still
> mounting my curious finger

He could as easily hold his blueness
> in flight arrested
> over crest of lawn or wave

You're right of course
> there are many dangers
> numbers of things to scream at

Don't ever my child
> be lured to cave or mountain top
> thinking dragons extinct

Though fire-breathing is outmoded
and daggering tails are cloaked
> dragons roam legion
> and no wise child thinks them extinct.

But dragonfly is nothing for fright
> in our setting of alarums
> don't exorcise this gentle excursioner

Praise him rather in silence and sight
> delight in this quick blue vision
> which really and truly can't hurt.

Part 4

Honor Card

Five by seven, aged brown,
it confers in fine penmanship
privileges on Miss Eddie Young
for her good scholarship,
Spring 1902, McElhaney's Academy,
the academy a note now
in someone's history
of Major Erath's county.

She was bright and had good bones,
now gone to earth, and heavy hair
that lasted almost long enough,
and in 1903, too poor to stay
left the academy
with contempt for her father
            who couldn't pay
            couldn't manage a hen and chickens,
            squandered what little he made
            on books, the only things he owned
            or wanted to, and read
            driving a borrowed plow
            on a rented farm.

And from the womb was angry
with her mother
            young wife birthing to season
            who widowed, dragged her brood
            to unwelcomes in ten spacious counties,
            and finally child-freed, spent decades
            in someone's spare room waiting death
            to come like a dark bridegroom
            and he did and found her sleeping.

And fifteen, their firstborn,
she my mother left
whichever rundown farm
where cotton never made
     furrows what they were
     and weevils rampant
to work for money
selling in a general store
and buying there almost her wages:
     the gold bracelet delicately chased
     apricot mull for dress so lovely
     it stayed sixty years unfading
     in her mind, and tortoise comb
     to become the lavish hair.

This of course is long ago,
and finding honor card
of her abandoned school
in her abandoned house,
I conjure by this relic
this once girl
most recent to me old woman
who wheelchaired counted hour by hour
'one two three ten,' beginning again
a hundred times, knowing such numbers
get no honor cards
nor starting the alphabet with *k*;
who screamed at thoughts
meandering like a buried river
in terrain of her dying brain;
and cried at her one good hand
gauzed like a boxer's for her jerking
from her flesh
unwanted intensive cares.

Contemptuous of her pooring
        lavish beyond right heritage
and of her passiveness
        betraying her right character
and angrier at herself
        than she ever was at anyone,
she tried again and again
to escape her paralyzed world,
restore brain to order, body to use,
but numbers were random
letters lost
and motion only dearest fiction.

Frustrated
she raged at this old woman
unable to please the ghost
of Mr. McElhaney or God
and certainly not herself.

I like to think her now
beyond rage, terror, tears,
beyond need for forgiveness, forgiving
turning young, light,
in raiment bright as apricots,
soft as mull, her hair splendid
beside Berenice's, her wrists
supple and gauzed only by gold,

and in honor and God's grace
moving sure as stars
radiant as constellations
easy in Zion
and easy too in self.

Recital

This new year's day I'm full of resolution:
today I take up the piano.
Hanon and Czerny will carry me back
to my thirteenth year, my stiff fingers,
rigid left hand turning supple as snakes.

My family fled to distant bedrooms,
I shall play the *Fantasy Impromptu* through.

It isn't easy: my fingers bend
to polishing silver, even subtle chases,
and to requirements of wools, delicate
at hand-wringing, but chromatics,
the first ones, stop me. I repeat

where there is no repeat. I repeat,
and bedroom doors close noisily above me.

And here in my living room
I try again: this time with a running start
my left hand almost makes it, rigid
third finger moving out of memory
as I summon up the curious legend
of fingering, where they go,
what the black keys require:

suddenly one door closed behind me opens:
I become her that I was
before hand-wringing was invented,
before silver knew any of tarnish,
the girl who conquered the two-part,
no, three-part inventions:

I am the girl in the pink net recital,
my petticoats taffeta smooth as silk,
my rose velvet sash perfect in its bow,
and my piece is last:

my freckles translate to flush
as the sweet hush of gardenias
mildly askew on my shoulder
wakes the piano to fragrance
and I step in grace to the keyboard

just after Marybeth Wyatt's botched Beethoven
and Frank Demerson forgot *Kinderszenen*,

and with perfect touch of memory,
my fantasy soars impromptu
in this turning year as above, behind,
closed doors open, awed by my sounding
this mystery of resurrection.

After Music, My Father

After music it would be dusk
and he would be waiting me
freed from tyrannous keyboard
lysoled against my contagions,

freed from scoldings
by Miss Cross who stood
metronome wary, ruler in hand
under the languid Christ
companioned by Beethoven
deaf to my violations
she too keenly heard
and shamed like leprosy.

Dismissed
I'd come running
through her garden,
a rainbow of irises and crocuses,

come in grief for time
my measures couldn't keep,
lamenting melodies locked
forever from my fingers
too awkward to uncode
the misty code of Schirmer.
My parody of music mocked my ears,
and clumsy and unmelodious
I ran to him as to love.

In the swift dusk
he waited innocent of Mozart,
untouched by Bach, unschooled in masses,
his only music one song, a whistling

his lips awkward as my hands
couldn't really make.

Leaving the garden
where Miss Cross instructed me
'God walked' and I fled in terror,
my father and I drove
from my lesson long as dog days
through streets darkling under trees,
their trunks already nighted,
drove home secure, happy,
innocents in this spring night

measuring its time
to take away this gentle whistler
of almost a song
quickly, irrevocably beyond home
beyond daughter
to whatever lessons of his long home,

abandoning me to this lesson
longer, more scolding than music
and to searching always
as in frightening gardens
where there are—must be—messages
coded more secretly than Schirmer
and even farther from my decoding,
and where neither father nor God walks.

Going with Gravity

Our hill glitters
treacherous in its sheath
honed of this sudden storm,
and like some petty god
cornered in a warm haven,
I peer from house toward ice
and her who will go to school
down a hill no car
can take but to disaster.

I watch her unsure-footed
slide and fall,
books scattering like marbles
and cautiously redeemed
as she moves sidewise
against slope
turned shrill as Everest,
her familiar world coldly betrayed.

My vision fails her face
though I know its look
reddening now to more than cold,
perplexed by this grotesque walking.

Then she begins again,
this time better,
and takes the slide
books in arms
going with gravity,
trusting inevitable fall
as much as Augustine, less hopeful
of grace than Calvin.

Going beyond my sight
she slides still imperiled
but guarded by knowing, learning
by movement how expectation
eases even inevitables
and reckoning of puny forces
can suffice to break
if not to counter fall.

Lesson: Tom

I like the scene:
she's six, bewildered of worlds,
knowing and not knowing
bewilderment, possessed
enough to practice at home
the worldliness of school

teaching her sister aged two
who's bewildered only
unknowingly, is gay
in haphazardy, much in control.

The lesson is reading:
a list of words recited
none too exactly
by the exacting instructor.

'Tom,' the student says
of all words.
'No, no, this word is Susan,'
the teacher repeats.
Her student doesn't believe.

'Tom, Tom,' the student declares,
knowing all words seen
as Tom now and forever,
word without end.

I've heard her declaration so long
I almost believe all words
like her Tom
a sacred syllable

and find this word, others,
puzzles in letters I know,
sounds I've heard,
meanings I understand
are beyond understanding
by letter, sound, sense

this curious pedagogy
teaching this knowledge
of believing one thing
and knowing no thing
nothing at all.

Dream Dogs

What beasts are these
come in black near-morning
hounding you
from drowsy sheets,
your eyes suddenly wide
quick feet urgent running
in dark to my bed.

'Dogs' you say
plunging my way.

Turning this night
I've heard your turning
restless, then running,
my sleep bayed back
by beasts almost at heart
and good at dark pursuit,
tracing by scent
more subtle than blood

though nothing of four feet
hunts as my beasts do.

Waiting their charge
these ominous hours
I've watched the garden,
its jasmine silvering
under the stingy moon,
its sweetness standing
against dark barks
stalking groves on the lawn.

Better than flower
as stand against dark
is your heavy sleep,
your head light on my arm
and staying till dawn
the dark animals
roaming our nights,

my beasts baying, vexed
almost beyond scenting
by the foul fiends born
of your six years' dreamings.

Girls after Ceremony

Thicket separates drive their car takes
from where I hide seeking clothes
and listen as these girls arrive chattering
senseless as jays. Middle-aged
and familiar of grave ceremonies,
I know their camaraderie, survivors'
surprised laugh after last rites
that says of a contemporary's dying
'yes, we endure, come safe from death simples,
skilled hiders from grave seeking.'

They're high school girls, this carload,
and death, swift, mysterious, come
to one of them is new to them all:
to her this noon entombed,
to them witness to syllogism
that all girls are mortal
though non-Aristotelians, they're logicless
enough to feel immortal.

Yet as they chatter, she touches them
and will in dreams, in memory
when a head turns a way they recollect,
a quick girl stoops to retrieve a comb
fallen from bright hair, when a laugh
sounds like one they can almost
place, and then placing,
they'll think of her in her new place

and come to know how they lost
this noontime maidenhood more fragile
than hymen. Somewhere far back
in heart learning mortal marriage,
they'll hear her saying 'yes, you endure
a while, meanwhile I hide waiting darkly
seeking,' and some syllogisms they'll discover
do persuade because even a generalization
can be particularly true.

I gather my dry wind-spun wash
to spindling basket and thread my way
to drive where she my daughter waits.
I look to her come from her first grave,
her friends now carred, carried away,
and will listen and try to hear whatever
it is she finds unable to say.

Pentecosts

"And how hear we every man in our own tongue?"

Acts 2:8

Our neighbors talked with God.
Every meal was Pentecost,
even littlest towhead shouting to ceiling
as flour gravy jelled to paste
and house cats battled devils.

At table before uncurtained windows
they prayed through hungry summer,
sibilant voices calling at meals
predictably as muezzins. In our house,
table wasn't set for the guest at Emmaus.

Then fast as they arrived here,
they fled the rented house,
mattresses a Jacob's ladder
atop their overfilled car.
'To preach,' my mother said,

'called to Pecos. Likely
they heard a jackass bray.'
She laughed at them
as we watched my father
gathering from hedge row
their messy leavings.
I gathered their leavings less easily.

Their God's ghost haunted, unknown,
unanswered in my catechism.
Scared by their bold rejoicings,
worried by mother mocking,
by unchurched father, my unknown self

was left confused by their noisy
mystery, ministry,

am left yet to wonder at prayer as silence,
presence as absence, belief as doubt,
doubt as belief, and to hope
this cloud of unknowing
is a pentecost too, an evangel
of disquiet, quiet, and the true.

Bells of Ireland

In a field I find them—
bells of Ireland, perfect,
graduated as carillons
stems straight as aspens,
and their colors are hers, reds
bright as cardinals in prime
and luminous as fine glass.

I cut, cut, cut, scissors
snapping like turtles
as my arms stretch
to embrace these marvels
and I run flower-heavy
looking everywhere for her,
run beyond forsaken world
to garbled fields,
think myself lost falling
as from a steep yard
falling far to find her

and I do:
not amid spindly asphodel
but as once she stood
content
watching her flowers
ringing to spring.

She is not old
or sick or dying but young
and laughing at my odd blooms
born of dreams.
She reaches to my arms

no longer tired,
takes these rare flowers,
and holds them easy in her spirit.

She touches my face, calm
with wonder
at her garlanded in love
and of world bright as prime,
sweet as light,
sudden as resurrection

and at her touch I wake.

Uncollected
and
New
Poems

Migrants

Inner-City Scene: Fort Worth

1. The Old Woman

In her present, little happens
but the past is an open book.
She reads its pages again

and again. No page records
last night's attack, and cheerful,
she turns today to a long-ago page

about a marriage where she finds
her husband's praise for her many gifts
and his good counsel in whatever it was

she thinks she once did, could now
should she choose. Most worn page
holds children playing in its lines.

Harmony rules her nursery
where change never intrudes,
no hurt injures, absence is fantasy.

These remarkable loving children
aging half a continent away
rarely leave this page, but if away

telephone every Sunday, dead receiver
linking distant voices to her distant present
bring ample news for a new week

of porch-sitting. Like the front page,
her news varies little day-to-day
though names she invokes never change.

2. Yard

Next door, the couple who'd never much liked
one another don't now. Evenings their voices

quarrel like jays. Mornings they take silent turns
sweeping walks, raking the garden, anything

to escape the crowded house. Two people fill,
overfill it, and take it—whatever "it" is—

out on the grass. Once "it" was children,
a son, two daughters, their wings

clipped short to keep them aground.
But feathers grew back and children fled.

Now no power mower cuts low enough to stop
the daily mowing, the grass crew-cut,

weeds scalped to roots by these rites,
mowers noisily fuming the neighborhood

with the furious cutting and flailing
familiars for years.

3. The Black Family

Whatever else they're lively,
these adults, children all kin
though blood lines are obscure.

One motherly sort tries a few flowers
but her plants encounter war—
oil cans, grease buckets, beer bottles,

remains of Kentucky Fried tossed
to seed in once-flowerbeds and lawn.
Decibels soar in this yard,

house where loudest radios never
conquer the many voices, countless barks
of dogs hungry, fecund, unlicensed.

And there are cars—dismantled, always
in repair, their private parts
a Stonehenge boldly circling the city lot.

Sometimes a car is put together,
speeds away, returns with others
to home there today. Meanwhile

garbage grows wings, radiators patina,
puppies and babies open shut eyes
to all wonders about them,

energy breeding, life living itself
as perpetually lively, lucky
to bring forth these rarest blooms,

this vortex aswirl with the human,
with animals, daisies, stock,
stubborn lantanas ignoring how hard
growth is in this hard ground.

4. Guanajuato

Only the Tovar children are citizens,
could vote were they the age.
Their parents, their most extended family

transplanted here from Guanajuato
("where the mummies are") work, make do,
pay taxes, carry their green cards

or lacking these, get taken back,
spend a night or two in Nuevo Laredo
and then return to this alien place

turning into home—they'd expected
only money. These transplants
plant—their children, flowers flourish.

Althea bushes, beds of vinca,
tall gladiolas parade on this homestead.
Even the youngest Tovar knows two names

for every flower, translates as needed.
It often is. But parents dig in,
don't give up, are catching on to a tongue

they'll never think to think in.
When the old woman next door
tells her latest news,

the parents listen, understand
there's no need to know her words.
The children know her vocabulary

but her grammar of age is alien
to these citizens rightly claiming
the promise of their young world.

5. Nights

Nights are loud in her wreck
of a house. Old trees scour
its frame, scrape last paint away.
A screen springs loose,
a window raises,
and there's another sound
that never stops.

She hears it every night
calm or windy, and listening
for it, sleeps restlessly.
But she doesn't scare.
Mornings she tells how her heart
acted up, the ambulance came,
and a hand fed her oxygen.

But this night, this hard hand
holds air away somewhere
in a faraway place she strains
to reach but can't.

Bedclothes tumble and her gown.
She wants to say "I don't wash much"
but speech holes up, hides
under this weight, this smell
that makes her feel bridal,
all her connections tearing
as wires, clothes, touch jumble
at this intrusion probing secret parts.

Next morning on her porch
she talks of the night long ago
when coming home early,
her husband surprised her.
But she knows she's a chapter to add
to this story today if her fingers
could find the right page.

The Tovar children hear, see
new bruises as old marks, and bored,
can't wait to flee to play.

dos semanas en Cholula

1. casita over the burial ground

nights their noises wake me, these
ancient ghosts prowling, spelling
in lost words intruders on sacred ground.

i never see them—others have—
but by day find their signs,
shale shaped to arrow at my door,

my papers shuffled, covered with marks.
i'm told their feet fit the narrow steps
of pyramid i see from my bedroom.

the indian woman who cleans, cooks,
does my wash, laughs at my turista
spanish never mentions them, claims

them as kin though she's native,
sings in an ancient tongue, moves up,
down the pyramid never looking.

i've little cleaning, washing, ironing,
mostly eat out, but she's always present,
and no cock crows them home,

these spirited spirits never still,
always quickening to life
in this conjured present.

even my tourist pass bears new symbols
scratched atop official seals,
old omens with no known translation.

2. dog day

nobody's dog, she's everybody's.
handout here, there on good days.
she always takes these gifts, grateful,
tail wagging, awkward. touch she takes
gingerly. *quesadilla* she's called
because she likes them best
but she eats anything. has.

this Sunday, church atop the pyramid
ringing early mass, firecrackers
greeting some saint's day,
i see her lying, legs running in air,
constricted throat allowing no sound.

then she recovers a bit, tries walking,
back legs dragging, tail limp.
then the agony comes again, fierce
and her last. she'd have been easy
to poison. eater of everything,
she'd have cleaned up all the arsenic.

her death is quick, efficient
not counting the pain. mass now
will be beyond confession. i wonder
if anyone did, will. i should too,
might have claimed her,
got her through customs,
helped her learn a meaning for *home.*

i didn't. no one did. stiffening now,
this corpse no one will claim
claims my yard already aswarm
with flies, their hungry buzzing.

3. neighbor to the pyramid

the casita is flat-roofed. butane
sits atop bringing agua caliente,
a stove that cooks. out my window

pyramid mountains, its seven and more
stories yet untold, little tunneled,
their meanings locked away, secure

in darkness black as deepest tomb.
i keep to my house, am no climber.
mountains enclosing the plain

confuse directions, and i can't tell
east from west, feel lost
on this earthquake-prone land.

my casita is safe relatively.
floors don't squeak, but no house
shuts out these ghosts who bumble

my world, blowing pilots,
raiding butane, jamming locks,
garbling in dead tongues, dry mouths

that nothing lasts, pyramid only survives
shaking earth, the past, this present.
then the floor shifts, books tumble,

dishes break, pier-and-beam giving,
as house moves toward a place
i can't see, name, grasp.

Boy with Dog, the Pan-American

This is no country for pastorals
and this boy's no business here—
no trestle with cactus fruit on board,
no iguanas swinging upside-down
heads scraping asphalt
back legs wired together.

What this boy's doing
is walking his dog—
this improbable act—
a boy walking a dog on a leash
no Kennel Club sort
but graciously long
tied to a collar that holds, won't choke,
and dog is determined not to break.

Smart, this dog? Maybe.
Scent tells him if diving buzzards don't
about the highway, the ruts in the burro,
carcasses of dogs too many to count.

But this dog isn't counting.
Safe, comfortable, he pads along
easy in his curious role
in this curious idyll—

a dog and a boy barely taller
than the dog
walking along the Pan American
where speed triumphs,
iguanas swinging in a child's clutch
never wave back,
and pastorals are rare as shade trees.

Francis in a Texas Yard

Baked of dust more lasting than mine,
he stands garlanded this April
by hackberries, pecans, a redbud,
wreathed almost eyeless by leaf buds,
choired to by bees, his feet
amid petunias that think it's summer.

Molded from Mexican soil
and displayed, sold by the hundreds
from highway stalls, this Francis
never walked Assisi, never will,
brick-based now in this prairie yard.

No stigmata show, his hands, feet
unpierced by swords of light Giotto saw.
Birds on his head, hand are clay.
Real birds ignore these birds
as saints might this crude relic.

But in spring greenery
or against winter's brown lines,
it pleases, reminds me—
no saint nor like to be—
of his life, birds, legend, canticles,
of Brother Wolf, Sister Death,
affirming in this alien geography,
time his ministry, joyful minstrelsy.

Migrants

They arrive unannounced,
no phoning ahead, no reservations
for check-in at the usual tree.
Then they set out, scout
this season's menu,
expect hackberries, some nectars,
are pleased at the stand of wild onions,
pokeweeds holding on in late summer.

Always too, secure as under glass,
are the earthworms, other earthy sorts
these quick, hearty fliers favor
on their stop-in at this hub
to refuel, enjoy a short rest.
Their morning flight is a red-eye—
August for all its warm welcome
won't last, and their destination
is the new spring a hemisphere away.

Their reds, greens, yellows
briefly decorate this useful place
they rely on, trust for a layover.
Rare here as ivorybills, they're wiser,
and sun-up, they'll head due south.

Come late March, early April,
they'll drop by heading north,
these meteorologists who know
where, when they want to go and must,
who for years have counted
on this Texas stop and the tree
that always takes them in.

Tour—Lascaux, 1957

After the long drive from Amiens,
truncated Beauvais, we reach
this earliest so-called *cathedral*,
this limestone cave rich
in inscrutable altars, meandering
cruciforms of paths, wall drawings
fixed on calcite and easy to see
when the guide turns lights on,
uses flashlight as pointer.

Above, steel doors opened briefly for us
are shut to hold out July heat,
the cave cool, temperature kept constant
as for centuries it was
before this *Sistine* was *discovered*
by four French boys trying to rescue
a dog that fell in a hole.
They fell too, these schoolboys,
and like Alice, found a Wonderland,
this place painted over centuries,
sealed away for millennia.

The guide leads us by narrow halls
to our stop, a rock hollow
large as drawing room, an atrium
where animals abound, parade,
these many alert, poised for something—
            no seeing what—
majestic, beautiful,
            some now extinct, others extant,
            one or two the guide labels "fantastic."

Then we go on, descend single-file
through low halls
to reach a small room or two
with few drawings, but spoiled

by the first grand room
we expect more than smallness.

The path continues to shrink
till we reach the cave's end,
its depth, floor steep, slippery,
space a premium, ceiling
so low we stoop to save scalps.

In this constricted space,
wall space is dear,
darkness a presence
despite the few lights
the guide turns on the only scene—
        the bird-headed, stick-figure,
        penis erect, his bird wand
        lying below his right hand,
        and the animals—the mammoth
        disemboweled and dying,
        the unhurt rhino walking away
        from the mammoth,
        from the only human here
        whose only weapon—if it is this—
        is a bird-headed wand beyond reach.

We walk away too,
follow our guide along
the steep paths,
by small rooms, across the big,
but only the path is lighted,
no second glance
at what we've just seen,
the well scene, strange markings,
the great room's animal kingdom
living now in memory.

Heavy doors open, we return
to summer, the suffocating car.
Tired, elated, we're awed by this place
lasting like a fly in amber, so strange
no one knows much of it,
understands what it means,
        not even our guide whose dog
        fell down a hole one afternoon
        and who with his friends,
        fell into this masterpiece, mystery.

Ramses: The Texas Stop

No priestly balms
prepared you for diesels,
the Mayflower flatbedding you here,
the gold parabola shrines
along your interstate progress,
high-rises taller than pyramids
monolithing over every polis.

"Play it as it lays," you hear here—
    new words, new characters
    for your old axiom.
You reigned decades, saw the new,
the old in Egypt and beyond
as you ruled, relished power,
did what you must to keep it.

Boater of the Dark Nile for millennia,
you know its secrets, know yourself
for what you are, a colossus
coming apart at the seams.
To help resew them, fix the fixable,
you come to this place, display yourself
as lasting pharaohs knew, know to do,
this display in life, in death the means
to tribute, gifts you seek in this New West
with no papyrus, no feluccas,
its only pyramids "schemes,"
Horus here only a hieratic sign on "coins,"
your god buried in tomb-dark "pockets"
with no altars, no believers' offerings.

Yet here too, ceremonies greet you,
greet the few attendants from your vast court—
    priests, astronomers, servants, concubines,
    wives, even Nefertari—
your palace now is this "museum,"

but ignorant of muses, you puzzle
at this shrine, its "holdings" mostly
these wall-hanging "paintings"
of no gods you worship, no king you know,
and with few statues, none grand as yours.

Craftsmen were yours to command, and you did.
Less to more they did your bidding.
You remember one, the master-sculptor
presenting this sculpture you live in,
who spoke of "the divine in your countenance."
Over your long life, rule, you heard much praise,
mostly from speakers praising their celebration
of you, your godly beauty, majesty,
but you never mocked them.
A pharaoh never laughed,
rarely smiled at the human
but you knew, know what you lived,
learned about trust, distrust.

Yours were, are "skeptical ears"
your court, generals, wives said
except Nefertari, who without hearing
understood your wishes,
never wished her words on you,
always gave you comfort,
a feeling of something like joy.

You remember too an astronomer
from far to the east who visited your court
and spoke of something you thought
might be true, that the world always
promises "new worlds" rife with
chaos, order, hope, loss,
the very stuff of life, its very mystery.

By day this Texas temple is busy, noisy,
unroyal, the many people, none dressed
for court, talking, pointing at you.

But you learned in your crib how little
court dress can hide the vulgar.

But by night, you love this tomb,
only a guard or two sleepily checking
the necropolis to keep you, your court,
its treasures safe. From windows, skylights,
you study this Texas sky, see the evening,
the morning star, know where Horus
will rise, set, and always, you thank him,
pray to Nut, Isis, Amen, the many
who gave you lifegifts,
and pray to Osiris for his deathgift,
your eons in his calm, unending kingdom.
You think too Nefertari, who taught you
of what here you hear called "love."

Watching these stars you can't name
brighten, dim, mostly you thank yourself
for your life, your learning, the memory
that help you discern what you were, are,
help you recognize the fugitive, the false,
and enjoy this lasting presence you are.

Neanderthals in the Gobi Highlands

The area covered by the Neanderthalers included the
entire Old World, from Indonesia and Central Asia to
Africa and Europe. . . . Evidence of their technical and
artistic accomplishments [and] their religious beliefs is
good reason for assuming their intellectual potential was
in no way inferior to that of their descendants."

Hogarth and Salomon, Prehistory

TV reports their possible presence, rumor
of occasional descents from highlands
inhospitable but safe. Mongols tell of
such sightings, usually at dusk when a man
with hunter's eyes comes near enough to see
their camp, the people, their tools, tents, cattle.

Other reports, unconfirmed but not disproved,
mention family groups of twenty or so
of various ages moving alert and watchful
to remoter regions. No animals accompany
these groups. It's doubtful cattle, horses
could survive such altitudes. Some Mongols hold
Neanderthals track mythic beasts
many here believe in, some have seen.

Only one Mongol, a trader camped at nightfall,
reports a meeting. He found the visitor shy,
perhaps afraid but curious if wary. Bifaces
were exchanged for pins, a handful of beads,
a flint scraper for a coil of rope.
Exchange made, the Neanderthal left
walking backward with care for his barter,
eyes always fixed on the story's teller.

Most agree such stories prove nothing,
yet sometimes smoke on far horizon
suggests a campsite, and some evenings

when wind is right, sounds from the heights
drift to the desert. What the sounds, songs
mean is a mystery. A few Mongols
think this strange music is hymn-like
suggesting fear of the unknown.

If so and if animals inhabit the highlands,
and if Neanderthals fear, are wary of unknowns,
of us, our lowland ways so that pins, beads, rope
remain curiosities, then these few ancestors
may survive, elude our cameras, probing,
and our weaponry more cunning than flint,
more deadly than bone knives.

thinking of *the potato eaters*

muse

chiton would drape most gracefully
but she'll come whatever dress required.
corsets may seduce or bikinis beckon.
her flesh fits either. she's seductive as hell

subtly firing a few good clues
till things freeze over,
and she's kind to lapsed heretics,
always offers hope of the given line.

but her worship is demanding,
our leaf-eating of little nurture
and her fiction mostly fiction
though she always has worshippers

and what do we gain? not her love,
charity, but maybe a word, a hook
to cast for the durable phrase—
enough to sell our souls for

gladly. were she Mary Misercordia,
chiton would shape to cape,
a shelter warm and protecting
but she only entices, gives no comfort

yet claims postulants and should,
these flagellants of the word,
believers in the perfect line, lines,
who exist for her, this myth,

and believe and don't
their fictions can come true.

Interview with Stephen Spender

"How does it feel," they ask,
eyes bright with thirteen years
of questions, "to be a minor poet?"

Decades past thirteen and still questioning,
he—poetwise—answers obliquely:
"I've a friend," he tells them
taking notes for their junior-high paper,
"who's a friend of the Lady Margaret.
She says, my friend who knows the princess,
'Only a princess knows how hard
it is always to be minor royalty.'"

They stop notetaking, look up, laugh,
as he does too, easy with hard questions,
uneasy with academic sorts, pedantic questions.

Their question does have substance,
is generously serious, takes account
of what they've learned of reputations.

"And you," he asks, "how does it feel
to be young?" They've not thought about it:
it feels like they are—they're sure of this.
They fumble his question, their answers
cumbersome, prosy. "You'll be surprised
one day," he says, "by a mirror,
your hair thinning, gray going white, skin pruny
when inside you're still you, the same person
who at thirteen asked hard questions."

They have their thank-you exit ready—
"When we think continually of those
who were truly great, we'll think of you,"
one says. They're blushy and funny

like the English schoolboys he knew,
was. "Don't misjudge," he tells them.
"Read truly. Remember Herodotus
writing that Homer 'carried myth
to its vanishing point.' My lines are better
at foregrounds," he says, "but minor poets
can be good critics, especially of the self."

Karen Blixen's Museum, Copenhagen

This discreet place becomes
its picturebook setting
in a picturebook city.
Poised toward sea and green hills,
this house was her port
to sail from in hope,
to sail to when needed.

Now it's home to her furniture,
amber carvings, photos
of what in best, worst times
she lived, lived among and knew,
and lost save for Isak Dinesen's words,
tales creating what, how she saw,
how her world was, is even now.

In this house, the Kikuku smile shyly
in soft brown prints, look almost at home
in this incongruous geography
of endless iced-in winters, unending nights,
of short summers with days so long
the sun barely nods to the west.

Now the Baroness too may be almost
at home here as storyteller wasn't
whose best loved birds weren't gulls,
most coveted crop wasn't rape,
and whose once-upon-a-time voyages
led to places, persons, work,
a life, another home she made, loved,
lost far from the land-locked Baltic.

Beginnings

for Ilze Skipsna Rothrock—1928-1981

how to start by beginnings;
this is the essential grace, favor;
how knowing past
    a Baltic zone, its low land opalescent,
    old port city keeping as amber

maps an unreclaimable country,
her Latvia, Riga a star-fix for navigator
    coming to unplotted frontier
    with its innocent, ominous prairies

and how learning mystery in exploring old
and in exploring new
    now and constant self newly tongued
    to strange vocabularies, disordered grammars,
    and hourglass sands running, shifting
    as they always do
one keeps faith and by faith brings
the past to the possible present.

if graced to beginnings, one wealths
the present, always the frontier to learn
    so to joy in tulips' hardy welcome
    to home with succulent kitchen,
    pussywillows vased on a writing desk,
    these branches of birth custom;

    to joy in motion, words, seeing, say,
    a crouching Venus, marble subtle as flesh,
    or a Bellini Virgin, her beauty
    a sanctuary at home with holiness;

to joy in books gathered as legacies
for fortunate heirs, and in fiction
crafted to life by a gifted hand
and secured in mortmain estate
durable as opals, amber

and always to joy in love, a love,
and always to be friends with essentials,
the loneness requiring beginnings,

accept as joyful mystery
loss of each second, every life
redeemed in sacrament of being.

how to start by beginnings
is to know grace.
even minor witnesses to this miracle
marvel at their good fortune,
how rare it is, she was,
how endearing, enduring.

Colette at Père Lachaise

"At last someone who speaks French."—
                    Colette, of a cat in America

This day becomes the place
gray rain washing alleys of tombs
going awry
where grave families lie
garlanded by rotting leaves.

The day discourages visitors,
only us here and a custodian or two
half-heartedly raking leaves,
but there are cats atop the monuments
still as statues
or dashing, rain too much,
toward shelter—where?
I move my mind for wondering.

Then we find her place—
Ici Repose Colette—
and her dates but no angel
except this cat gray as the day
and enduring as rotting leaves
who, wary, watches us
but doesn't speak

though she must hear
his scratchy crooning language
seductive as the French of lovers
visiting Héloïse and Abelard.

This cat wants nothing of us
except our leaving
to leave him alone with her
waiting leaf-mealed, listening.

the man in the VA hospital

mornings he hobbles around
checking Waco's second-hand shops
that sell him prints, old photos,
a scrapbook of somebody's life.

by noon he's ready for the p.o.,
his weekday trade in catalogs,
postage for packages he sends
every week—to a sister a long way away,
to her children so scattered
they never can find his address.

afternoons back home at the hospital,
he "cheers up the boys" saying
God knows what. it doesn't matter.
they only half listen, better half
turned to TV, but they know
how he is, how they are, how it is
when no prosthesis ever fits right.

nights if he sleeps,
in-heat mares buck him awake.
good nights he lies abed trying
to string together thoughts
about legs, how two help arrest falling,
about how words turn into poems,
lines on canvas limn a world.

nights his chart labels "bad,"
he balances at a make-shift easel
jabbing at dark with layers
of paint hottest July can't dry.
flowers no botanist knows
bloom in vivid colors crippling,
their dyes bleeding before his eyes.

come dawn, the nurse checks,
calls housekeeping as he hides
paints, brushes, washes up,
hopes syringe she brings lets him wake
by ten to begin his day, its regimen
an order against chaos, his victory
in holding on, a sort of sorting out.

thinking of *the potato eaters*

"to bring *life* into it"—Van Gogh

how bored they must have been
after the long day in fields
to sit for this man at his easel
demanding them in this, their own house
to let the kerosene lamp burn down
just so, to be still, hold
these unnatural poses, rigid heads,
backs, hands unmoving.

and they've things to do this evening,
each of them, even the man
offering the potato towards his wife
and thinking of bed, next morning, work.
they're all tired, especially the woman,
arm raised, wrist, hand straining
with the kettle's iron weight.

did she dislike the lighting,
mind his making her skin look like
a dirty potato, her nose wide as a snout,
turning her white bonnet gray?
did she protest when he fixed her arm
in midair as if it had rested all day,
this arm that dug, wrested tubers from the earth?

or was the posing welcome, a respite,
the quiet hospitable even if backs hurt,
visitor intruded, his mutterings, Bible talk,
brushes, palette knife smearing the canvas
meant to bring them, their meal to life
or so he promised? did she wonder
if he thought of backs, kettle's weight,
their work, the tomorrows in wet fields?

did she ask what he thought of them?
what did he think?
did anyone speak of, at this meal,
were the potatoes done, seasoned?
did he eat at this table
before, after the posing, painting?
was, is the meal a sacrament,
what does the/a painting mean?

the painting says and doesn't.

exhibition

"look this way," canvases say,
"look at it this way. see!" they command
flaunting their pigments, dyes,
their brazen conception
in eyes, mind that looked, saw,
and like Spinoza searching for God,
found in "the predicate of substance"
all proof belief requires.

knowing dyes leach, lie,
she searched plains, arroyos, heights
for form, color, shadows to fix
on canvas flat, taut within frame.

her canvases avow, parade their limits,
revel in them, their surfaces and hers
whose hands stretched, mixed,
brushed what eyes saw as a way to see

the Jack-in-the-Pulpit preaching
his purple prose of begots,
a ladder going nowhere,
a church, its pilasters thigh-heavy
like a woman urgent to birth,
and late, the black door closed
to the patio stark with light, shadows.

another canvas says, "i'm yellows
and pinks," asks "what am i?"
and lets the riddle go, answers
colors, being, seeing suffice.

canvases invite, guide, define,
open eyes to what is, its/her reality,
what form is, the integrity of seeing

adobe, flower, skull, desert
pristine in bareness, swelter, life,
the quiet angled patio
black door testifying
to light, dark, predicate
of the maker's being, its being.

Mondrian at the Supermarket

framed on housewifely form
rectangles and lines
ordered as panes of glass
montage down aisles
of staples, luxuries at eye level,
geometric meats so cunningly cut
only the color betrays their origin.

it's as impossible to know
thoughts of this Mondrian-clad
shopper pushing her cart,
choosing goods for her needs

as to know how his thoughts
turned him from windmills, mums
to abstracts, forms, perimeters
as neat as nature isn't.

any of many realities is, can be
one-at-a-time satisfactory—
        a woman shopping,
        a painter's colored planes.
both have their place,
but juxtaposed, these two
collide in a strange mating
dissonant with questions about goods,
their uses, purposes—

why in the world—
        or maybe why not—
is this flesh-hung Mondrian
walking aisles at the A&P?

Studio—Lascaux

He didn't have north light,
any light except the glow
from burning fats cradled
in fonts he found in the rock

but this light sufficed,
showed wall surfaces, terrains,
rises, falls to fit fleet hooves of deer,
the large black cow jumping,
   forefeet aground,
    the back legs fixed in motion,
and beneath the cow,
on the lowest wall good for colors,
the ideal space for a frieze—
   the horse leading four colts
    small as eohippus, shy as okapis.

Where a meter or two of smooth rock
rounded, he profiled bulls, the unicorn,
outlined, lined within to evoke
bones, the swell of tensed muscles.

His ochres mixed to reds, yellows,
a hint of mauve, and stirred soot
let him find the black lines
of the mammoth, strokes to make it
breathe, grow restive to spring from image
to life. But his hair brush, paints
held it fast, caught all these many beasts
more lastingly than any spearhead or trap,

hands drawing in these animals
to the cool sanctuary of his dark studio
where for eons they've lived,

do now, breathing, waiting,
ready to walk, leap, land, wound,
be wounded but not die,

secure in this domain, their lives
the gift of his hands, dyes, his sight,
his light shining in this dark place.

an academic poem

you stumble fumbling to life
beating with too many stresses.
in reality you've one just reason
for being, the metaphor hiding
amid your randy, unsorted syllables.

you want pleasing rhythms,
some assonance, tidying each
perverse, awkward verse.
a plague of tautology, you speak
amphigory when sense wants out.
your synecdoches are a pain,
and hardly more than analects,
you don't yet know who you are
though you're sound basically
and there's your metaphor.

you long to make yourself heard,
exchange shady doppelgänger
for your true eponym,
craft metonymy to fit your likeness.

cutting away, taking on shape,
and kenning yourself to knowing,
you groom your wordy illogic
to oxymoron of your metaphor,
throw away loose ends, try anaphora,
and fashion by this regimen
best ordering of your best words
so that you stand to be and to mean
more than you are
and you do.

instantly you forget
the stumbling, fumbling memory
that set you going, untidy birth,

those messy sheets, bloody types,
practicing quire it took
to set you singing.

come to your majority, you're independent,
self-willed, and paged, you speak
yourself as if immortal
and expecting reams of eternity
because you are sound and make sense,

wild oats beginning cultivated
to character of your artful being,
irony firming bones, hyperbole
dieted away, litotes muscling,
true persona lying in metaphor
fleshed exactly as you want it.

The Terrible Peaceable Kingdom

Santos

Impervious saints stare from retablos over hearth,
Clare with the heart, Francis and his quiet birds,
Jerome and the dark skull, gentle lion.
I've watched these santos over many seasons
seeing their constancy as no part of me,
an Ixion wheel-spinning for confusions
about love, God, false gods, and more.

Wide Mexican eyes of these saints seem
to watch tableaux of life here—coffees, teas,
tonics, books, persons served before this hearth
as at a mock altar. Sometimes our watches meet—
their eyes depthless in folk artists' watery paints,
mine buried in cataracts blurring surfaces,
shifting depths, heights out of plumb

though when our eyes meet, I remember
these saints were human, hurling once
on bone but spinning too on a wheel
turning toward the true, the real,
and by grace and favor of the divine
and the majesty of their humbled hearts
came to be friends of God, to love
the divine, the human, and our world
in its loveliness and not

to become exempla to us
unsainted, ungraced
but sometimes pervious
to their mime, its reality, its hope.

Babel on Sunday

For years I hadn't recked this lore
which I remember as ringing
in bright loneliness of new tongues
speaking without answer to once-kin
gathered near abandoned ziggurat
on desert no longer mined for bricks.

This bright day, sun warming
the garden warning of spring,
she my daughter comes Sunday-schooled
home babbling of Babel
and would know its meanings.

Of old teachings I say,
we try to speak to others but can't,
syllables missing meaning
and teasing as dustdevils, so we hear
as the deaf hear birds, in silence,
longing, and we feel lonely I say.

It fails, my explanation,
and Babel-weary she turns to toys.
Our meeting fashions no brick, not one,
the Genesis story still true, a presage
of now. Her questions want answers,
my words phrase soliloquy.
and sly as syllables, she slips away
to her world real beyond my words.

Sly too, I pursue discourse
with myself, empathetic to babble
as this house, our mutual shelter,
transforms this luminous afternoon
to broken tower spread on the desert
where we move now as always
solipsists confined to speak
in tongues defying translation.

Metaphor

Her first season so named,
this fall is marked by drawing
dying leaves in vivid colors
and hearing why (one reason)
colors change.

"Jack Frost comes," she tells me,
"and paints leaves my teacher says."
She's told this before
(and will again)
and believes it and doesn't
and this time asks
(and will again)
"Is it true?"

Even at five, one knows truth
worth a query
without yet seeing truth
as a path of eight ways or more
but seeing a path going at least
two ways headed to places
too faraway to see.

"It's true in a way,"
I try my old answer
(and will again).
"What way?"
"A way of speaking, a metaphor," I say.
I tell her metaphors are ways
of speaking, seeing likenesses
real and not—frost colors leaves
so we say Jack Frost comes by night
to color them one by one
and this is true in a way.

Through all her childhood and my life,
I expect to be saying of that
worth but beyond knowing
(this is my body, this is my blood),
"They're metaphors,"
as she and her questions
are a metaphor for love.

poor heart

poor heart,
center now of nothing at all.

Vesalius removed sense
Aristotle generously bestowed,
Freud and others cut out feeling
centuries alive in your hammering.

what remains is eccentric
beating in a space
dark in flesh, blood
always pulsing except
for short rests, the final stop.

you merit tears
but weeping is dated
and laughter ludicrous
considering your state,
you messy, bloody thing
pumping for no reason you know.

some i know wish, poor heart,
you lived in gentler times
willing to grant you a legend,
but dumb—if you are—
know times change,
theories come, go.

know too how sorry, sore
at heart, tugged by heartstrings
some are and i am
at your impoverishing and ours,
poor heart.

The Terrible Peaceable Kingdom

"No one can love God who has not perfectly loved one
of his creatures."
—Margaret of Navarre

Leashed, caged, carried, they arrive
cats of many colors, furs, voices,
dogs of breeds known and unknown,
a borzoi hounded by malaise,
a bull-dog wheezing in his fatty realm,
and the old ones, their dis-
ease tolling a quick easing.

The young come too, in health
for shots and accommodating
to our wants for grooming, shaping fur,
bobbing tails, ears,
declawing to fit our sanctuaries.

Waiting, owners talk, form
a humane society
at the neighborhood vet's,
speak always of pets
more human than humans
to comfort our human cravings.

But animals waiting don't chat,
visit, make new friends,
these lions and lambs
lying together in terror
in this peaceable kingdom,
its harmony born of needs
theirs and ours
for love, to love, be loved,

our love partial, conditional,
waiting discovery of wholeness
and like all our other loves
        (who but a saint can perfectly
        love any one of God's creatures?)
fragmented, so imperfect
only a loving god can forgive.

Waterscape

1. Such bond and carrion bondage
dates to a time I barely remember
I decades back, fourteen
and he my brief senior.

The lake that day looked
winterhard but month was August,
its ice-smooth surface an illusion.
The boat we sailed was beautiful,
its hull bluegreen like the lake,
its sails whiter, more quiet than clouds.

Mid-lake the boat stuck
        we knew the lake low
        but not that low
sand locking keel
in a vise we couldn't open.
We jolted stopped
to come men by rights
in the dissembling lake
though boys still to make
games as we could.

2. Who said it I don't know now
but one did: that we walk the bar
to find how far it spanned
        we'd no purpose
        for this knowledge—
        it was pure as far
        as knowledge goes—
and we did that
he north, I south,
the boat equator
to our soundings.

We called each ten steps
looked back to boat
and each other.
The third ten I only called,
and turned to see arms flailing,
sinking swift as Icarus.
I ran to where sand gave way
and schooled by his example
watched what I thought
I couldn't change.

3. I'd like to remember I knew him well,
was marked by his short dying
but I didn't, wasn't.
I knew him as he knew me,
a boy among many boys
at summer camp
and I've become what I was, am
meant to be
middle-aged, respectable,
almost prosperous, not quite happy.

But I remember him
as I watch my sons and so myself,
boys fair and dark as men
present and to be,
no reason I know
one should be swallowed, one not.
His lot—I speak of fact—
was north,
mine south,
his land gave way, mine didn't.

4. To say I read God in it all
is to say nothing
for I know nothing of such mooring.
Whatever it is or was
is so long ago it's unlikely

others survive to remark event
to me as layered in memory
impossible to peel away
as for him to be freed
from his waterlogged
sand-plastered fate
or for me to be free
of this bond I can't explain,
can neither forge nor forfeit.

Aftermath—Christmas Morning

The revelation a memory now,
in house, in us comes this silence,
every gift given, opened, all cards
mailed, read or not.

In separate rooms, the youngest
try new toys, build, tear down,
start again, games with others
saved for afternoon.

Older children are off to peers
to compare booty from home,
unknown kin while we wait, await
without want the coming dinner.

Angel wings outspread presage
the cross to which this child
just born must soon make
His calendar way,
His shepherds, magi absent then,
who worshiped His birth
in time of joy untainted,
His star lighting the heavens,
earth to proclaim this miracle.

Day, night, our Christmas lights flicker,
suggest the tree's lines but barely disguise
its dying greenery.

In its way, this aftermath is right,
our separateness, comparing,
waiting testimony to our condition
even as it's possible to hope
the joy we knew at midnight
might lighten, enlighten days,
help us understand what in us

led us to honor His birth
and will bring His last hours.

Let something of that first joy,
of cattle, shepherds, kings
kneeling to a child be real, whole
in us and beyond analogy true.

Prelude

What coming forth is this from rocky berth—
man born out of desert tomb,
no wanderer on sands like John,
but dead, buried rising to walk earth, teach
by body, presence the truth of His teachings?

To this birth what witnesses? The divine,
angels easy with mystery, and the human,
the Marys to see, Thomas to doubt, touch, honor,
and others whose stories we have.

Believed, this untended birth taught
rebirth, a miracle like and not lore
of an Osiris, a Dionysius—His showing forth
to reclaim a human life interrupted one Friday,

this birth from grave not greenery prelude
to His later coming when skies will dazzle
with a new sun as Heaven bends to earth,
Christ come in kingliness so that we
at His third epiphany might believe, honor.

To Christ on the Second Birthday

I address this profane poem to holiness beyond my ken.
The first birth I can understand, having seen births,
love the lore of cattle breathing to warm him,
kneeling each Christmas eve, remembering,
and the death itself easy to understand
even if the cross is obsolete, but dying
is the same, the pain, some words, seven perhaps,
to ponder, not forget. But his second birth

is the mystery. I can believe the impossible
but believing, wonder on that morning,
how he found things, himself certainly different.
Perfect man, perfect God in the first birth,
at the second was he human too, having died
and being free of death? Only divine, he must
have seen our lovely, lent world with new eyes,
less easily found beauty in quince aflame
on dry branches or the Judas hung with red buds
but making no fruit.

Except for Lazarus, his other miracles are easy,
a child's play of marvels until this second birth.
Here I'm bewildered trying to place him
in our fallen world, am left to wonder
how he, human in form but other than human,
saw those he knew, loved.

But what mother, what manger, what simples,
what comfort in his new world of only grace?

Afternoon Coming

We weren't prepared for this. In the afternoon
dizzy with bottomless skies, all heaven broke loose.
Lounging in a comfortable chaise, sipping a cool nectar,
bantering with a summer novel, thoughts far from eternity,
we weren't yearning for holy splendor.

Brilliant birds supping wilted flowers dazzled
enough, buzzing of bees ample trumpeting,
light play on pool's top sufficient mystery.
Then uninvited, intruding in our welcomed time,
eternity came.

On some winter morning of sabbath feeling
we might have greeted holiness appropriately,
our needs, hopes shaping due courtesy,
our lives less contentedly earthward.

But this afternoon, this earth, this life sated.
In time of this showing forth, we turned
dumb eyes back to unholy books,
heard angelic songs with mute ears

as we rested easy in body, uneager spirit
while all heaven sang hymns to this one
come in love whom we in this indifferent hour
could not rise to crucify
or offer nectar to assuage thirst.

epiphany

late, disordered as out of Troy fallen
i travel uncertain of direction
born in a new country bound now to old
my walk unsure, gait shuffling
certain only of voices inward, outward
discouraging, doubting.

nor i no magus,
the name only seasonally apt,
lacking royalty, wisdom,
born truly of my century
to believe nobility dubious,
wisdom relative,
certain only of uncertainty.

to thus come

bringing no gift
despite my traditional start,
myrrh and the rest traded early
for necessaries of travel,
frivolous presents by then long lost
      ball bounded away in winter wind
      that uncaged the bird singing its freedom,
      out-of-season cherries rotted
      perhaps to birth as tree, fruit
      in some season i won't see.

so to come
with no birth gift

but like a child in darkness
of my thousands of nights,
arriving no longer young
weary from the long journey
it seems i could not make earlier
to this slovenly place,

come of no desire save necessity
and offering nothing,
poor in goods, good, love, spirit,
rich only in need
a child in innocence might take
for wonder, worship, awe, love

to come then with little faith
except hope of the child's hope
for the hopeless,
charity for the undeserving

a late dull non-magus
so weary a manger looks like comfort,
a place to rest where faith might be born.

no-fault divorce

Children's Games

Some come by Ben Franklin's
good invention teach how to stay
in bounds, not step on lines, and win.

Others teach morals about dropping things,
falling & the fall from spinning too long
too fast in a circle (as if we had a choice!)

But the really dangerous games are those
with pointed endings
like "home free" & "safe."

Children never are nor parents either.
We're all skating on the pond
Brueghel showed us, taught us to see,
      sun shining, pond people-filled,
      and the ice ready to crack.

no-fault divorce

only the toaster works.
everything else is on the blink—
even the blender, which noises to life
only for 'crush' and 'slice.'

once-upon-a-time, argument
could have been made for repair,
for fixing the irreparable. it wasn't
as papers with official seals confirm.

both sides, the documents record,
want civil justice,
swear to no-fault either way.

an accountant waiting in the waiting room
might on court order appraise
this estate, fairly assign gains, losses
even to the blender's failing,

but petitioners seek no appraisal,
petition only to dissolve
this four-legged monster
their high hopes once made legal.

given to assessing high hopes,
any accountant would value
this lawful being, the improbable
geography it wanted to homestead,

a naive place where blend cycles
always worked, manna was daily bread,
and love the durable good, goods.

briefly once, this monster lived
to lumber to this fairness,
but no polestar was right, no compass
adequate for the long journey

to what was likely to be a mirage,
an inviting land where troths, say,
were kilned carefully as Dansk,
which handled recklessly can craze,
break, shatter though its shards,
some say, never disintegrate.
in fact, legend holds they're insoluble
and like memories, live forever and ever.

to the girl about to deliver

you're partner in this
with this unknown you've known
for months in its growing,
lazy turning, kicks, tosses.
what you want now is the birth.
you count on this charge
you carry to free itself
to its own need-rich world.
but you must—should—know
you won't be home free.
you should know too by now
how care goes, what time this child
will require. nine months help
prepare you a little for this.

now isn't a good time to reckon
other separations less flesh-tearing,
less sharp to body than contractions
but in time you'll feel these too,
learn their rhythms, remember to pace
your strength, breathing.
Lamaze is a help, teaching you
about inhaling, letting air go
when you think you can't
like the first time this child
dives from the high board,
drives the car alone,
misses curfew and it's midnight,
won't speak at breakfast, washes
hands clean of you and the wrongs—
these are many—you stand for.

you'll learn to pace these things,
breathe like yoga tells you,
and with the best of luck
you'll find the sacred syllable you need
and labor to believe in it,
have faith your faith works
for more than only you.

but now you can't wait
for birth to be over,
yearn to put on your thin body again,
carry yourself like you always have
though you won't even if clothes
closeted for months almost fit.

something more is happening now.
is it your heart? how can you know?
but there's something new,
something you didn't know was there.
what surprises is that you know
about this before you have time
to learn anything at all
except your relief
that this child decides now
is the time to be born
and he is.

Saturday before Dying

"That same Saturday Simone told Mme Closon that
perhaps she would be able to eat some mashed potatoes
if they were prepared in the French manner, a purée like
her mother made."

Petrément, *Simone Weil*

Finally with the starving,
the mind recedes, its passion spent,
baptism no longer debate
or hunger the sworn creed.
Sometimes in this receding
just before all longing stops,
body comforts
and memory mothers.

As a dancer might remember
balance at perilous point
or a musician how hands once
were forged to marvels,
she whose vocation was morals,
who subtled conscience to a peril
of balance and forged her iron ethic
on her body, turned child
of Mnemosyne and remembered food.

Like a Francis warmed at last
under piece of cloth and at peace
with father as with Father,
or a Teresa happy to walk any road,
anger at divine mud all dried,

dying this martyr thought of taste,
remembered once-pleasure in food
before mind knew much of arguments
to raven against the body's need.

Death was kind, his sleepy arrival
letting her keep a dream
of a fine purée, its pleasure
even when the past it belonged to
is lost to war, persecutions
she escaped but in conscience, couldn't.

Electing to starve as millions did
without choice, she fed at last
on gentle memories, and gracious
Death called before she roused
to discover mind no longer knew
how to tell her mouth to sip,
her throat to swallow.

present

now only flies covet
this brief plaything
lying belly up
its green-yellow breast
beaded with feeders
its claws clutched to air
ruby throat at an angle
of no breathing thing.

a quick look could take
these feathers for fallen leaves,
not for what a well-fed cat
wanted to catch, toy with,
bring home and she does,
this stillness of no interest
and not worth eating.

this present waits at my door—
something even the cat won't drag in.

The Ordinary Woman

She was your ordinary woman,
maybe taller, bigger-boned than most
but maybe not. But "ordinary."
On any chart, that's where she fit, fits—

weight to height, education, income,
voting, other socio-political actions,
courtship, marriage, children,
duties to parents, their illnesses,
her surgeries to take away the faulty—
       buried wisdom teeth excavated,
       extra bone in one ankle excised,
       a pre-cancerous womb cut away
       and, to be safe, both breasts.

Whatever the feminine form,
she was heroically unheroic,
never protested except by ballot,
wifed a house open to many.
Cooktop, oven show she served
lots of hot meals; worn sheetrock
testifies she tended many children
imprinting dirty hands on cleaned walls.
She cared in more ways than one
for a husband who most days
came home promptly after work.

But the house gave out, not disrepair exactly,
when her last surgeries came.
Then children set out to imprint
their hands on their real worlds.
About then, parents died,
and literally, statistically too
she became the "older generation."
Her husband never returned
from a weekend business trip.

About this time,
this absolutely ordinary woman
who fit every chart except ones
charted to measure immeasurables
like spirit suddenly discovered—
she was no explorer—
her self:

this total surprise
for this most ordinary of women.

You might think she fed,
fasted on memories. She didn't
even if memories of good times
and bad were vivid.
She opted to go with the good.

Then this perfectly ordinary woman
made another—for her—discovery:
that home was where she was, is,
and home, she learned, knows has spirit,
her own and something more,

the mix of gains, losses a life accrues,
and something else not charted,
this "else" better than a limited partner,
than housewifery, mothering,
than polls of losses, gains.

something about the mystery
of happiness with what is,
the comfort of accepting
the ordinary that is,
she was, is, is always to be.

Back

Racquetball does it. "Something pulled"
you say. You move like an old man bent
by laborsome travels, your body dramatic,
a text of pain. I become your partner,

this house our court. I think of Sparta,
the old kings remembering Troy,
its splendid wounds, and Helen listening,
serving the drink forgetfully flavored.

I'm good too with flavors, favors. "I'll rub it,"
I say and I do. You lie still, bedded
with your ache. My fingers turn subtle as silver
fish darting, hiding in flesh shoals.

Muscles give to this school, move easy as waves,
and all at once, I turn your Helen,
my hands swimming the great barrier
reef of your pull. Touch the restorer.

We've known many Troys, can sing lots
of sad songs, but epic in scope, we've more
than one theme. We surprise to find
this one still remembered, its flavor,

seasoning, savoring of backs favoring us back.
Fallen walls rebuilding themselves
to first splendor, all crumbling done,
back in place as if by Circe's best simples.

And like Helen, I listen, am glad for pain,
endurance, old love come these late days
to our court alive with leaping fish
so iridescent their silver shines like gold.

gym

1. volleyball

we were flat and worried,
especially when we saw
Cynthia rounding gym clothes.
her curves were real,

not the handkerchief-linen folds
shifting on Bettyann's chest
when she forgot and lunged for the ball.
no one envied Bettyann.

Cynthia was another story.

when she volleyed,
we thought about grace.
when she moved,
we sensed the mystery of motion.

the hour we had to spend
in gym never made her red-faced
like me or freckled like Mary Alice.
in the shower we spied

on her fairness, read her body
like a sacred text. "but she's fast."
Bettyann confided, "boys are after her."
abashed, we heard, reproved, despaired.

"nice" girls we waited, hoped
to learn the naked truth of what
we'd become. we never did.
when we grew to bras, gym suits

still didn't fit, volleyball left
our skin a mess, our hair
matted with sweat and oils.
mothers worried, assuring us,

themselves our "awkward" stage
would pass even if arms and legs
remained "a little ungainly."
the best we could do was watch,

mime her envied moves, and sternly
forecast justice in her unhappy ending,
our sad hearts lamenting
her high drama was never to come
to even one of us.

2. team sports

no one was ever last.
Mrs. Robertson saw to this.
after captains' quick first choices,
some of us never among them,
"enough," she'd say, "captains
can't take all day deciding,"
her swift swats to bottoms
sending unchosens to team A or Alpha.

she was "tough" we all agreed,
the bold girls adding "as hell,"
and she was always fussing,
scolding our lazy badminton, soccer,
our volleys. she scorned
our serves, returns, defense.

we hated team sports,
even the captains, the chosen,
and she made every one of us play.
"tough" about rules, her rule,
she swatted to life face-saving teams
as if we didn't see what she was doing,
this balancing act of good, bad, indifferent.
none of us liked it.

but sometimes we forgot dislike,
how teams were made,
who we were,
and amazed ourselves,
called out, urged on "our side."

sometimes my side won
and i'd be proud
but she didn't praise winners.
"do that yourselves," she'd say,
dismissing us, calling in equipment,
ignoring that what she put together
we were amazed to briefly become.

3. physical education

each class she ordered us
to "suit out," answer roll
with "suited out" or "off floor,"
her grade book noting attendance,
periods, any irregulars.

but she seemed to have no periods.
she always wore gym clothes,
her figure proof of benefits in playing
every game created by woman, man.

but we didn't want these benefits,
were more eager to know about periods,
other mysteries like hot flashes,
greedy for news of what, who we were.

in ninth-grade wisdom we decided
Mrs. Robertson was "middle-aged"
and "too young." we were right.

in January someone noticed.
then none of us ever missed class.
come March, boxy jacket over shorts,
she didn't play our games anymore,
came on court only to show us a shot,
direct an arm as it ought to go.

mainly she kept score.
even losers never fussed.
we kept score too
but we counted wrong.

first class after spring break,
she'd shed her jacket.
we all agreed she looked good.
then the seniors gave her the gift—
        the cup engraved for her daughter.
before class we all signed the card.

as she opened the box
we clapped and laughed.
then we suited out
but that day she didn't take roll.

driving in the thirties

for them it would have been a long day
starting at three when he woke
whatever season to go to work

and she faithed to ritual of wife
rose to clean the spotless,
cook for us as for an army.

after the long day, humdrum work done,
done well, daily test of duties passed
till morning, summer evenings

they'd be consciously leisured
when we'd go driving, old Chevy
taking city streets to country,

nearby acres recalling farm ways, pleasure
in city choice, electricity, running water,
all conveniences, compared.

we drove roads so narrow Johnson grass
whipped the car, and i'd try to grab
a few burnished heads and did.

remembering this, i'm always six
going on seven those nights i'd grow
sleepy to rhythms of motion, sound,

their sounds, their silence saying
how much they accepted
the passenger in the back seat.

almost asleep, i'd see them,
heads looking ahead, their eyes
safe conduct through whatever dark,

and next morning i'd wake in my bed
to familiar sound of her sweeping,
scent of apricot pies baking "first thing"

before heat of day. she'd be whistling,
listening for his coming, late breakfast
warming now. when i was seven,

this world ended, no eyes able
to pierce the sudden dark. but before,
when dozing in the Chevy meant

waking in my bed, my world was sured
by love, no absence long, return certain,
these trustees of my estate bonded,

their charity lasting forever
so it seemed once to me.

Reunion

Mr. Bones we innocents named him,
this hanging man naked beyond flesh,
this show-and-tell for biology class.
Viewing him with dumb eyes,
we mocked his yellowed bones,
mimed dancing beneath his dangling feet
metal frame barely kept from floor.

He was a show, a death's head
telling nothing but names to us
young in flesh, firmly muscled,
unlikely kin to this primer of man.

This alum weekend
visiting with my remnant class,
the lucky ones who're only older,
I wander a strange campus,
walk in unknown buildings,
pass offices of no teacher
I know, wander in a maze
that once had plan
but hold no thread to the way back.

Seeing him in a classroom
teaching to other juniors,
I meet a friend, greet a prophet
whose prophecy is true,
time's seeking long ago
finding him, making him "it,"
leaving him no place
to hide his truth.

non-pro

three and ten is optimistic—
it's three and fifty and time
is running as my field gilds

with flags, penalties for holding,
grabbing masks, illegal
offensive procedures.

defensively off-side i drift
scoreless toward the sudden death.
though my team is only me.

i've played many positions—
guard, center, tight-end, place kicker,
linebacker, daughter, wife, mother,

slaved, unslaved before i knew
i was bought, come unbonded
but nothing's worked right—

plays were badly planned, foul
in execution, and overtime
won't redeem this scoreless game.

in this tv-colored hour
football lines are cheap trades
as life can be though it's slippery

and harder than artificials of turf.
but three and fifty's no metaphor
in this real, undaylight saving—

clock ticking, odds rushing
to dark as time runs down
to the two-minute warning,
the final time-out.

Driving Lesson

You're driving in the mountains. Landscape
familiar and not. "I'm hungry," you say looking
for a place. Pull-outs few, landfall as it is.

Then you see the space, small but enough,
pull in, brake against incline. Redwings
signal everywhere. Even one bluebird.

You unpack lunch, yesterday's leftovers
turned sandwiches. But fresh chips
and ripe cherries. Everything good, just enough.

You're satisfied, comfortable more
and less. You feel companioned,
extraordinary this. Then time to go on.

"Ready?" you say. No one answers.
Everything changes in this landscape
familiar and not. You look everywhere,

up, down, under, but you're alone.
Predictable that bluebird is gone,
but redwings too are fled,

little to picnic on in your leavings.
Now you know what there is to know
about feasts, fasts, how everything changes

even if sometimes you forget,
believe "once" "now," and startle
to remember "once" isn't.

You know too to go on,
look close for, to direction,
know not to stay braked

where you are, but wherever you go,
you hear what's racing, never brakes,
is always gaining on you,

this best teacher who brings
to graduation every student,
even the most forgetful charges.

Father

You're sick today and decades from young. Sickness
not serious. A virus, 24-hour sort.

But you're sick, old, want comfort
which is a child's thing. Then you know

what you want—something that was long ago
when you were child and sickness scared.

You didn't know a stomach could turn on you so.
What you learned too is how strong his hand was

holding your feverish head in his cool palm.
Your slops didn't sicken him, and stomach

almost calmed while your head rested
in his square Irish hand

secure enough to hold forever.
This is ages back, this sickness, his comfort.

You've not thought of his ghost in weeks.
None left now but you to remember him,

and you do and kindly and wish him here,
wish yourself that child, that once-miracle

though you know how to cope, accept
the wisdom of not telling longings

but wonder on, treasure—and you do—
the simple dress love can wear
and what memory closets.

leaving

this time too you carry away things

—cuttings, succulents, rooted stems
that know to grow where growing's hard,
will succumb in the kinless place
you're more and less settled in.

—and peppers too. you pack each kind,
hot, sweet, the temperate to toughened tongue.

—and always, something old, forgotten.
this time a quilt top a peace-making
old woman i loved pieced from shirtwaists.
she'd have been your great-grandmother,
is i guess as genealogists reckon.
i reckon more the knowing day-to-day.

—and always, the throwaways. brownies
in case the plane falls and you need chocolate.
an orange for good vitamins,
a dr pepper—you like these.

your packing argues
distance is a minor thing:
you can take the here with you.

my gathering says
distance is major:
you can need help, will need reminders.

but we glean only a meager harvest
that wouldn't make a meal,
keep you one night in the sierras.

at best, our rite reaps self-leavings,
a lore warming over how we were, are.
most, I guess, we try for something

we don't say: a letter home
that needs no posting. this letter
if we wrote it would speak of love,
trust, and our wish for safe journey
to wherever it is we each must go.

Love as Potatoes

I never thought of potatoes, brownies
as love apples, but they are on Tuesdays
when three boys heading home from school
make a quick stop at my house.

These boys, who ring the doorbell many times
and jingle the copper bell too to be sure,
enter in wrinkly clothes (no starch lasts
the day in kindergarten, second grade),
come with grimy hands once morning-clean.
Their hands with pencil marks, crayon stains
always carry stars, indelible "happy faces"
for "good" in reading, arithmetic, conduct.

Sometimes these hands have new scratches,
bruises no boy clearly explains, and always
these six hands, busier than brains,
host a world of germs though no one here
believes the germ theory or takes scratches,
bruises for signs of non-good conduct.

After-school hunger being scientifically proven,
Tuesdays I boil potatoes for George,
stir up brownie mixes—
    one for Landon, who likes pecans,
    one for Stephen, who takes his dough neat—
and since they like to "try" new things,
they have "surprises"—
    jellies (we're hunting the ideal licorice bean),
    cookies from Germany, France, the deli.
Sometimes these "news" please,
sometimes not. It doesn't matter.
We all know to count on the standards,
    boiled potatoes, brownies we trust.

These treats to eat in a kitchen
      where cats beg a hand-out
      and dogs are the clean-up crew
are a new aphrodisiac, powerful,
guaranteed to work, these potatoes,
these brownies, this rite, our mutual faith
Tuesday treats will be here—
      mine for them,
      they for me.

clocks

once
a clock i know
knew someone would come
each week to wind it,
help it bring this house
seven days of time

as its hands moved round
its face with Roman numerals
and its iron innards sounded quarters,
hours two earlier generations
heard in other houses.

now
the clock I know
is digital.
handless, faceless,
programmed to readouts,
it clicks minutes, hours away
in red numbers, buzzes alarm
to announce each morning.

when storms make light fail,
the digital stops. when power returns,
it flashes 12:00 until my digits
correct its disfunction,
push buttons for hour, minute, alarm,
decide between noon and midnight.

prompted by no clock, no calendar,
i think from time to time
of the brass key waiting
in the walnut case
and the person i knew who used it
each Sunday to assure
a week's worth of time

in this house when keeping time
mattered, storms caused
only minor disfunctions,
and overall, occasions
for alarms were few.

Return

If you surprised me this afternoon
touching icy lips to my neck,
clasping my waist with stiff hands,
I'd start, surprised, glad,
would hold you like life,
warm your hands, feet, cold body,
nourish you with drink, food
careful to avoid excess.

Knowing to the day
how long your absence,
I'd wonder at the hard travel
bringing you home,
and after you supped and I fed
on the marvel of your presence,
you'd tell me how it was
your sudden leaving,
how you called—think you did—my name
but there was no answer. So swift it was,
the ways things go with the heart.
You'd tell me where you've been,
news of this strange place, and I'd listen,
spelled as by Odysseus or other rare traveler.

I'd joy in your return, your words,
and you'd joy to be here, to know
how things were, you gone.
I could tell only of coping, making-do,
no heroics like yours. I'd not say
how you gone all turned make-believe
to keep back the sad, and we'd be happy—
our single wandering, making do over,
our lost times gladly lost.

Comforted to have hearts again,
we'd rest easy in their even rhythms
and we'd dream
    you that you were home,
    I that your dream was true.